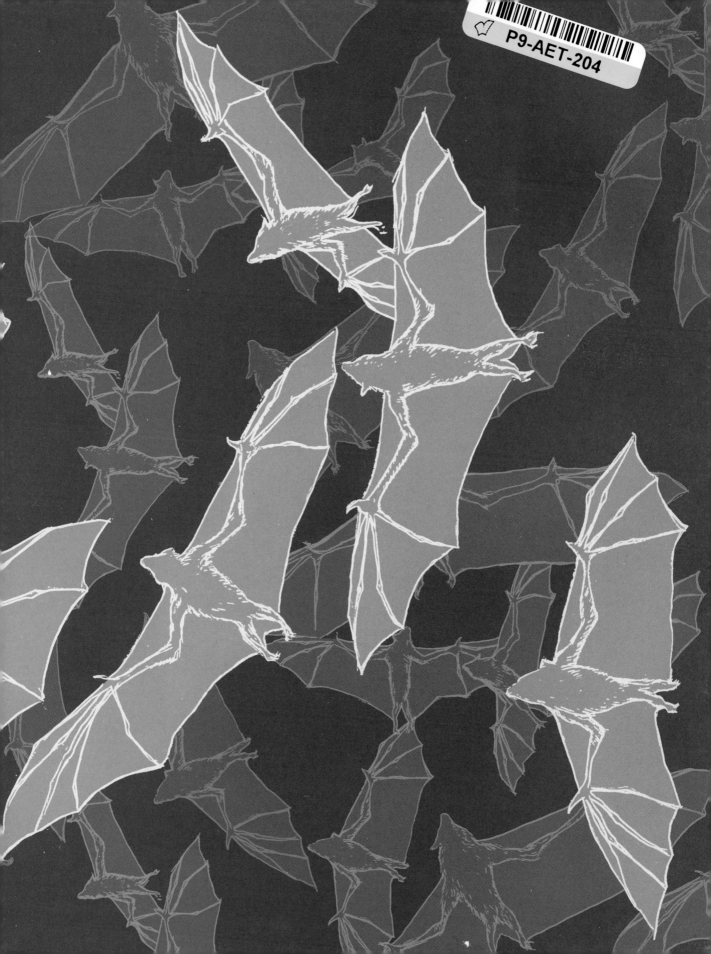
P9-AET-204

Hanging

with

Bats

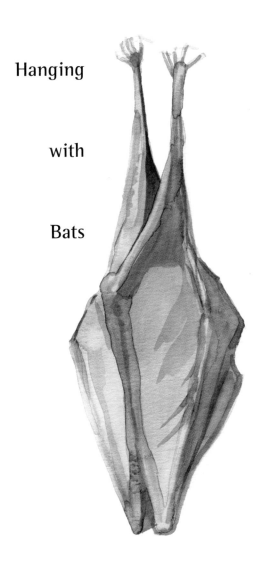

The lesser long-nosed bat (*Leptonycteris yerbabuenae*) feeds on a Plamer agave. More about pollen-eating bats on page 49.

Hanging with Bats

Ecobats, Vampires, and Movie Stars

Karen Taschek

University of New Mexico Press 🦇 Albuquerque

Welcome to

Worlds of Wonder

A Children's Science Series

Please see page 92 for more information about the series.

© 2008 by the University of New Mexico Press
All rights reserved. Published 2008
Printed in Singapore by TWP America, Inc.

13 12 11 10 09 08   1   2   3   4   5   6

LIBRARY OF CONGRESS CATALOGING-IN-PUBLICATION DATA
Taschek, Karen, 1956–
Hanging with bats : ecobats, vampires, and movie stars /
Karen Taschek.
p. cm. — (Worlds of wonder)
Includes index.
ISBN 978-0-8263-4403-8 (CLOTH : ALK. PAPER)
1. Bats—Juvenile literature. I. Title.
QL737.C5T37 2008
599.4—dc22

2008002076

Series design by Kathleen Sparkes
Book composition by Kathleen Sparkes
This design uses Warnock Pro famliy OTF 12/16, 32P3,
and the display families are Warnock Pro and Ag Rotis.

Contents

To John, patron of the arts
and especially of this writer.
Without your critical sense,
common sense, and financial support,
this book wouldn't exist.
Thanks and love.

Acknowledgments

Special thanks to Barbara French, biologist and science officer at Bat Conservation International in Austin, Texas, for an interview that gave shape and scope to this book, for access to her research on bat talk, and for the charming photos of Mexican free-tailed bats at home; to Dan Taylor, Bat Conservation International, for his wonderful story of life as a bat scientist in the trees and for the photos proving he really was up there; to Mike Bogan, Corrales, New Mexico, for his insight into the scientific process as it applies to bats; to John O. Whitaker, Department of Ecology and Organismal Biology at Indiana State University in Terre Haute, for his help on the complicated subject of bat evolution; to Gerald Carter, Department of Biology, University of Western Ontario, Canada, for his vivid and admiring descriptions of real vampires; to Paul Cryan, US Geological Survey, Fort Collins, Colorado, for his help on the subject of bat migration and the dangers of wind power; and to the University of New Mexico Press staff for making the press's Worlds of Wonder science series for children, of which this book is the first title, a reality.

EVENING FLIGHT

Flight of the Mexican free-tailed bats (*Tadarida brasiliensis*) at Carlsbad
Caverns, New Mexico, on a late summer evening. Sometimes more than
800,000 bats fly out of the bat cave but sometimes barely 8,000. If insects
are scarce around the cave, the bats will live somewhere else for a time.

CHAPTER ONE

Chock-full of Bats

Carlsbad Caverns, New Mexico

A Bat's Night Out—Catching an Insect Dinner

At Carlsbad Caverns, in the south of New Mexico, are many deep, long black caves made of limestone. Some of the caves are empty, dark holes of dripping rock—the drips build the upward- and downward-pointing fingers of stalagmites and stalactites. At dusk, the last bit of light fades from the entrances of the cold caves, and the blackness settles down for the night.

But one cave is getting ready to burst with life. Since late afternoon, hundreds of thousands of Mexican free-tailed bats have been restlessly moving about this cave. Dropping from their upside-down roosts on the roof of the cave, the bats begin to fly, circling toward the entrance of the cave and the twilight. The bats are getting jazzed for a night out.

The Mexican freetails will eat a dinner of moths, beetles, flies, and whatever other insects they can find. Since the bats sleep all day and are awake at night, from the bats' perspective, they might be looking for breakfast. In the bat cave, as many as a million wings beat the air, blowing out the musty, dank air. The Mexican freetails are really all wing: their wings stretch 11.3 to 12.3 inches (28.7 to 31.2 centimeters) across. The bats' bodies are only the length of a human thumb, and they weigh less than half an ounce, but when so many bats take flight at once, they create a live, whirling black tornado.

Up on the Roof
A colony of Mexican freetails
roost together on the roof of
a cave in New Mexico.

The bats burst out of the cave for 20 minutes or so, spiraling up into the sky. Sometimes just one huge group leaves together, and on other evenings several groups will go. A few tardy bats get up late and straggle out of the cave after the big wave has left. After they have left the cave, the bats break up into smaller groups. The bats shoot across the sky like darts, specks of black against hazy blue.

Mexican freetails aren't the only bats in the caves and skies of Carlsbad. More than a dozen *species* of bats live there—and one species of bat is now *extinct*, or has died out. The Mexican freetails live at Carlsbad only in the warm months, when insects are around, and then fly to Mexico for the winter. These bats get their name because most of their tail sticks out past the membrane, or skin, at the back of the bat. While flying, the bats can move this membrane back toward the tip of the tail, like an airplane adjusting its wing flaps.

Bats can fly like birds, but the bodies and wings of birds and bats are very different. Bats aren't a weird kind of bird, or flying rats, or Dracula in disguise. They are *mammals*, which birds are not. And bats aren't close relatives of rats. (Bats' relation with Dracula and other forms of the undead is discussed later. Also how bats are really related to other animals, like monkeys and humans.)

Deep in the night, the Mexican freetails take a break from their search for an insect meal, sometimes perching to rest in a tree. It's midnight and high noon for the bats. Three in the morning could be siesta time.

Finally, at dawn, the bats make their way back to the cave. They don't return in a huge bunch, the way they left—the tired bats fly back mostly by themselves. Mother Mexican freetails eat the most: on a typical summer night, they eat about 30,000 pounds (13,500 kilograms) of insects. These bats eat half of their body weight in insects each night.

The bats take aim at the entrance of the cave, fold their wings partway, and zoom through the cave's mouth, going faster than they have all night. The bats zip and dart as they constantly adjust their wings so that they land in the right spot.

Once in the cave, the bats go back to their roosts and settle on the roof of the cave to sleep upside down. When they need to, the Mexican freetails can walk as well as fly, although they often walk backward. The bats don't look like they could walk very well on their tiny feet, but in fact they are quite nimble. The bats gather

COWBOY CAVER Jim White, explorer of the bat cave at Carlsbad Caverns.

Meet Me at the Bat Cave: Carlsbad Bats and Tourists Clash

The Mexican free-tailed bats at Carlsbad Caverns have lived in the caves a very long time, although humans didn't record their evening flights until about a century ago. About 3,000 years ago, Mescalero Apache Indians camped near the bat cave, eating meals and drawing art—the Indians left behind remains of a cooking pit and grinding tools, and they painted pictographs on the rocks, showing important scenes from their life. The Mescaleros surely saw the bats, although they left no record of their thoughts about them. In those days, the Mescaleros had to think constantly about survival and probably had no need to go into a dark, musty-smelling cave. Other than the bats, not much possible food is in the cave—only some tiny white crickets and a few other strange insects that live in total darkness.

In 1901, the bat cave at Carlsbad was rediscovered by a young cowboy named Jim White, who had ridden the range near the cave for about 10 years. White and his companions knew about the deep, black holes in the ground here and there around Carlsbad. But no one had ever been curious about

Hanging with Bats

the caves until one evening, when White saw a startling event. "I thought it was a volcano," White said. "But then I'd never seen one. For that matter, I'd never seen bats fly. I had seen plenty of prairie whirlwinds during my life on the range, but this thing didn't move. It seemed to stay in one spot near the ground—but the top kept spinning upward. I watched maybe a half an hour, and being about as curious as the next fellow, I started toward the place." The bats kept boiling out of the hole. White tried to guess how many there were—he thought millions. In any case, a hole big enough to hold all those bats had to be huge.

White and his wife moved into a shack next to the bat cave. For years, White made exploration of the caverns, including the bat cave, his mission. But for a long time, few other people knew about the wonders of the caverns. In 1903, Abijah Long realized he could make use of the bat cave in another way: by mining guano, or bat droppings, for fertilizer. The guano mining took place only from September through March, when the Mexican freetails had migrated south to Mexico. Long blasted two holes in the top of the cave to haul out bags of guano.

One day, seizing an opportunity, Jim White took a photographer into the caverns. Usually White put visitors in an empty guano bucket to lower them to the cave floor. The pictures the photographer took finally got out the news about the bats and caves at Carlsbad. In 1923, Carlsbad Caverns became a National Monument, and mining of guano stopped in the bat cave. In 1981, the holes in the roof of the bat cave were filled in, and the Mexican freetails returned to those roosting spots.

Mexican freetails swirl across the
entrance to the Carlsbad bat cave,
beginning their nightly hunt for insects.

These days, the Mexican freetails need
their beauty rest because they are the stars of
their own show. Every evening in the summer,
human visitors come in droves to watch the bat
flight out of the cave. Gone are the days of Jim White,
when the guano bucket dropped off visitors to the caves
in a pile of guano. There they had to wait for the rest of their
group to be lowered to join them. People were tougher in
those days—now visitors to Carlsbad Caverns are lowered to
the floor of the caves in a speedy elevator that doesn't smell
at all, and people sit in a stone amphitheater in front of the
bat cave to watch the bat flight.

Just before the bat flight show begins, a park ranger warns the visitors to be quiet and not disturb the bats. Before the bats are finished coming out of the cave, some people get up anyway and clump up the steps and out of the amphitheater, talking. A small wave of Mexican freetails swoops down and darts just over the heads of the people who are still sitting. The bats miss hitting everybody. A few people are delighted by this close encounter with bats, but some cry out in fear.

And that pretty much sums up people's relationship with bats today.

Bat Ancestor

This bat fossil is from the Green River Formation in southwest Wyoming. The bat was an insect eater. Even millions of years ago, bats looked much the same as they do now.

CHAPTER TWO

The Beginning of Bats

Bats and the Dawn Horse

Evolution explains how an animal, like a bat, changed over the years, or evolved, to become as perfect as it is. Animals evolve when their *environment* changes so that they can find food, survive in the temperatures around them, and have young. The oldest known bat *fossil*, or rock version of a bat, frozen in time, is about 53 million years old. What's amazing about the fossil, of the species *Icaronycteris index*, is that the old bat is hardly different from today's bats.

Bats got their looks and lifestyle right a long time ago. All bats have the kind of wings, ears, and teeth they need to survive in the forests, deserts, and many other parts of the world where they live. When the early bat that became the *Icaronycteris index* fossil was alive, it lived alongside other early animals, including sharks in the sea and horses on land. Like bats, 50 million years ago sharks looked much as they do today. If you saw even a 400-million-year-old shark, you'd have no doubt what it was—*shark*! A frightening eating machine. But although the first horse, *Eohippus* (which means "dawn horse" in Latin), was walking around the planet 50 million years ago, it looked nothing like today's horse. It looked more like a weird dog with a long, thin tail and would have come up to about your knees. Even two million years ago, the first humans (our great-great-something grandparents) were still covered with hair and looked more like animals than people.

So bats hit on a winning lifestyle not as long ago as sharks but way before horses or humans. Exactly how and when bats evolved into what they are today isn't a sure thing, though. Dead bats don't often leave good fossils. Bats' bones are small and break easily, and so bat fossils are rare. A five-foot-long head bone from a *Tyrannosaurus rex* dinosaur is much stronger and much more likely to be preserved as a fossil. So the fossil record of bats may have missing links.

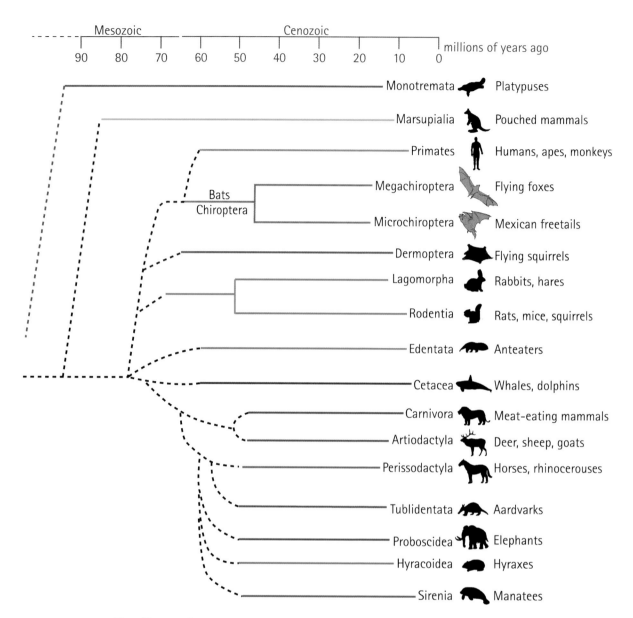

	Mesozoic		Cenozoic							millions of years ago

90 80 70 60 50 40 30 20 10 0

Monotremata — Platypuses

Marsupialia — Pouched mammals

Primates — Humans, apes, monkeys

Bats Chiroptera
  Megachiroptera — Flying foxes
  Microchiroptera — Mexican freetails

Dermoptera — Flying squirrels

Lagomorpha — Rabbits, hares

Rodentia — Rats, mice, squirrels

Edentata — Anteaters

Cetacea — Whales, dolphins

Carnivora — Meat-eating mammals

Artiodactyla — Deer, sheep, goats

Perissodactyla — Horses, rhinocerouses

Tublidentata — Aardvarks

Proboscidea — Elephants

Hyracoidea — Hyraxes

Sirenia — Manatees

THE TREE OF LIFE

To keep track of how different kinds of animals and plants are related, in 1758
Carolus Linnaeus, a Swedish biologist, invented a way to name them that can be put
on an evolutionary tree, with branches. The dotted lines to the left of the branches
show approximately when some of the animal orders split off and became different
from one another. The bats branch of the tree split off from the rodents branch
of the tree a long time ago, before the bats split off from primates, the order that
people belong to, and so bats are more closely related to people than to rats.

Hanging with Bats

Can Rats Fly?

Bats are part of a class of animals called *mammals*. To be a mammal, an animal must be *warm blooded*, or stay the same body temperature whether it's hot or cold outside. Not all animals can stay the same temperature—a lizard or snake that crawls up on a rock will soon be whatever temperature the rock is. All mammals have fur or hair, and mammal mothers feed their babies milk. Rats, bats, horses, people, and many other animals are mammals. Sharks are a weird, not-really-fish thing. We humans (and other mammals) haven't had much in common with sharks for a very long time.

But mammals are different from one another in many ways, as you can probably guess if you look at yourself and then compare yourself to a rat or bat. Bats are the only mammals that can fly. Millions of years ago, back before the first bat fossil formed, bats' hands changed into wings. Before bats had wings, they may have jumped from tree to tree, spreading their arms and gliding. Flying squirrels glide today, but they don't actually fly. Slowly, bats could have formed membranes between their fingers and developed the right muscles to power their wings. Animals evolve, or change, like this to get an advantage over other animals—being in the air to get from one tree to another instead of being on the ground could mean not getting eaten by another animal.

Many bats are small, furry, and move quickly, and so some people call them flying rats. But if you can get a bat to slow down and you look carefully at it (instead of pointing at a brown blur in the sky and shouting, "There goes a rat!"), you'll see that the bat doesn't look anything like a rat. Bats really are more like people, their closer relations. Scientists think that bats and humans evolved from the same kind of small, shrewlike animal many millions of years ago. (Shrews look like moles and have a pointy nose, tiny eyes, and short fur.) Bats live a long time, like people—one ancient bat in Siberia is 41 years old—and most female bats have just one baby, called a pup, a year. Rats live only a few years and can have a huge number of babies each year.

Bats in the Time of McDonald's

For a long time, bats have stayed bats—flying and with bat teeth and an airplane shape—but they have changed over the years into many different species, or kinds, of bats. Bats come in an incredible number of sizes and colors. Some have short ears, wrinkled faces, or spots. The bumblebee bat is the world's tiniest mammal, weighing just 20 ounces (two grams), but a flying fox may have up to a six-foot (two-meter) wingspan. More than 1,100 species of bat have been found, and the number keeps going up. Bats make up almost a fourth of all the species of mammals. That means if you have four mammals, one is likely to be a bat.

The order Chiroptera, which includes all bats, is divided into two major suborders: Megachiroptera and Microchiroptera. The Megachiroptera, or *megabats*, are beautiful bats. These bats have big, soulful eyes and long noses. The Megachiroptera are sometimes called flying foxes, and they do look like foxes soaring across the sky. Flying foxes may have wingspans of up to six feet (two meters).

The Megachiroptera bats all have a claw on their second finger, and most of them rely more on their eyes than the Microchiroptera, or *microbats*. Megabats eat mostly fruit or nectar, a sweet drink from flowers, and pollen, a dust that is needed to produce plant seeds from flowers. The megabats use their noses and eyes to find food.

DELICIOUS FLOWERS
The wings and faces of flying foxes, or megabats, are designed to help them find and eat fruit, pollen, and nectar. This southern blossom bat (*Syconycteris australis*) uses its long tongue to pollinate a swamp banksia plant in Australia. The southern blossom bat is a tiny flying fox.

have small eyes and large ears in proportion to their head size. Their faces often have strange lumps, ridges, and wrinkles.

MEGACHIROPTERA
have large eyes and long noses and look a little like foxes.

The Microchiroptera have small eyes and often have lumps, wrinkles, and ridges on their faces. Many also have huge, twisted, or strangely shaped ears. Most microbats eat insects. Others eat fruit, nectar, and pollen, like the megabats. A few microbats are *carnivores* and eat small birds, mice, frogs, lizards, or fish. Only three species of bats drink blood—the vampire bats. All of the vampires are microbats. Unlike megabats and humans, all microbats can use sound waves to find their food. (More on *echolocation*, the use of these sound waves, in chapter 3.)

READY TO HUNT
A Mexican freetail, a species of microbat, poses for the camera before heading out for an insect meal.

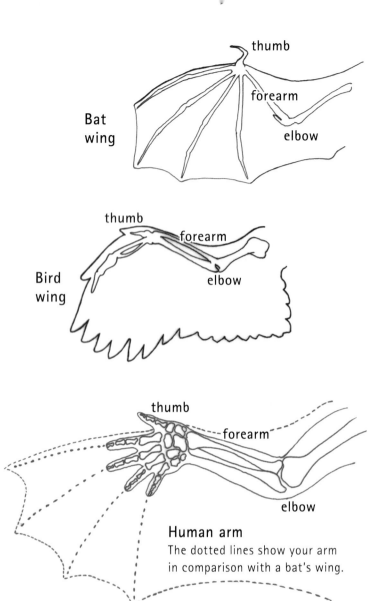

Bat wing

thumb
forearm
elbow

Bird wing

thumb
forearm
elbow

thumb
forearm
elbow

Human arm
The dotted lines show your arm in comparison with a bat's wing.

second finger
third finger

THE EVOLUTION OF ARMS AND HANDS

Bats and birds both have wings and can fly, but they are not close relatives. Over many millions of years, these animals came up with different solutions to the problem of how to fly. Bats fly with their fingers, and birds fly with their arms. If you look at the skeleton of a bat, under its skin you can see four very long fingers extending off the bat's arm. The fingers support the bat's wing membranes. Birds' arms support their wings. Bat wings are covered with skin, and bird wings are covered with feathers. Bats use their arm muscles to power flying, and birds use arm muscles and muscles in their sternum, or chest.

The word *Chiroptera* means "hand wing" in Latin. And that is what bats have done with their hands—turned them into wings during evolution. Bats' legs look somewhat like human legs, and their leg bones are much like ours, but a bat's thigh bones are turned 180 degrees, or backward, compared to a human's, so the bat's knees and feet point backward. This helps bats hang upside down, ready to drop into the air and fly.

If you look closely at a bat's wing, you will see that it is indeed a hand and arm—but the fingers, except for the thumb, have become very long and are covered by two layers of rubbery skin to make wings. The wings are much tougher than they look and heal quickly if the bat gets a tear.

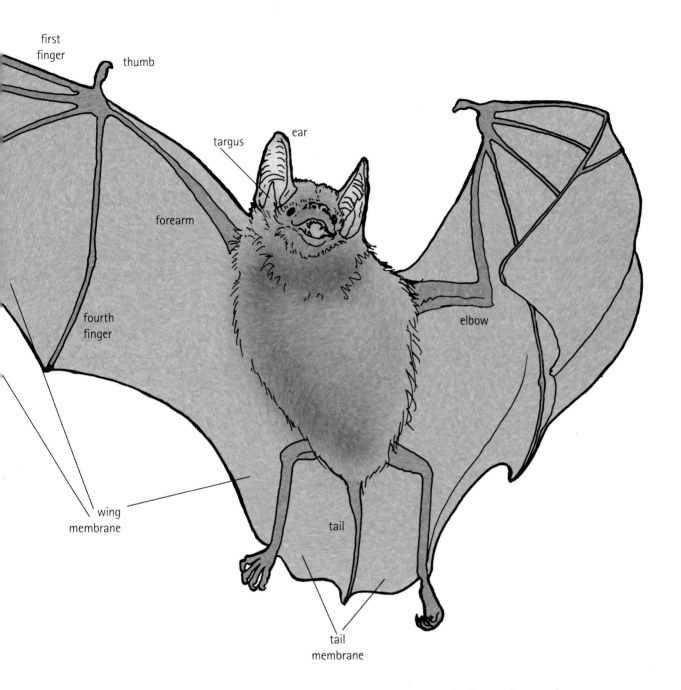

first
finger

thumb

targus   ear

forearm

fourth
finger

elbow

wing
membrane

tail

tail
membrane

The exact shape of a bat's wing depends both on what the bat is designed to eat and on how far it must fly for the winter to find food. Bats that eat insects have long, narrow wings, which are better for flying fast after insects and for flying long distances. Mexican freetails have this kind of wings. Bats that eat fruit or food on the ground, like beetles, and don't fly long distances have short, wide wings. With these wings, the bats can fly slowly and maneuver around plants in a crowded jungle or forest. Flying foxes have this kind of wings.

The Evolution of Evolution

In 1859, Charles Darwin famously described the theory of evolution in his book *On the Origin of Species*. Darwin based his theory on observations of plants and animals he had made on a trip around the world in his sailing ship the *Beagle*. For example, on the Galápagos Islands, off the coast of South America, Darwin saw 13 kinds of finches, small birds that eat seeds. The beaks of the finches were slightly different, depending on exactly what food the birds ate. "The most curious fact is the perfect gradation in the size of the beaks," Darwin wrote in his journal.

Later, Darwin took this as a sign that the finches had evolved so that their beaks were just right to pick up the particular seeds they ate. Finches that could eat well, or were well adapted, would have more young finches. These young would then pass on the well-adapted beaks to their young. Darwin talked about "survival of the fittest"—the animals and plants that could adjust the best to their environment would be the ones that lived and had young. Evolution is a slow process and usually takes place over millions of years.

Modern scientists took Darwin's theory further. Now changes in our *genes*, small packets of chemicals inside our cells, are known to be what causes animals

to evolve. But evolution happens by chance—a gene will *mutate*, or become slightly different, and that may change an animal, giving it, for example, longer fur that keeps it warm or a stronger wing that helps it fly. You can't *think* a change like longer fur or a stronger wing. You can't just decide you want your children to have bigger muscles, then you eat a lot of meat, and presto! Your children will have giant muscles.

CHARLES DARWIN
Darwin first described the processes of evolution.

THE VOYAGE OF THE *BEAGLE*

Artist Conrad Martin made this painting of the HMS *Beagle* in Tierra del Fuego off the coast of Argentina and Chile, during his voyage in the *Beagle* with Charles Darwin, 1831–1836.

Fifty years before Darwin came up with his theory of evolution, French naturalist Jean-Baptiste Lamarck came up with the idea of the "inheritance of acquired traits," which said exactly that: what parents did to their own bodies would affect their children's bodies. Lamarck proposed that giraffes stretch their necks by reaching higher in trees for leaves and then pass on those stretched necks to their young. Of course, this doesn't happen.

Lamarck seemed to be dead wrong. If you dye your hair blue, your children won't have blue hair. But now it seems that Lamarck might be partly right. The science magazine *Discover* reports that scientists took fat, yellow, sickly mice and fed the mother mice a special diet. Those mothers' babies turned out to be thin, brown, and healthy. This outcome gave scientists a jolt. According to Darwin's theory of evolution, the mice should have looked like their parents.

These days, the news is full of stories about how kids are getting fatter and fatter from sodas and junk food sold at school, in the neighborhood, and on almost every possible street corner. But the danger may be bigger than anyone thought—if *you* get fat from eating too many Twinkies, Ho Hos, and Mallomars, your *kids* might be fat too.

SHARING A MEAL

A Peters' dwarf epauletted fruit bat
(*Micropteropus pusillus*) perches upside
down on a fig, watching an incoming bat.
(An epaulette is a fringed shoulder pad on old-
style military uniforms.) The bats eat figs and
other fruit and then spread the seeds, helping
new plants to grow. These bats live in Africa.

CHAPTER THREE

Life as a Bat

Where Bats Call Home

Bats live almost everywhere in the world, from your backyard to rain forests. To live in such different places, bats have evolved the right kind of wings, feet, ears, and other body parts to survive in them. The result is a wide variety of bats that look very different from one another.

The megabats, or flying foxes, are sometimes also called Old World bats because they don't live in the New World discovered by Christopher Columbus—North and South America. Megabats are found in Africa, Asia, Australia, Europe, and some islands. Microbats live on every continent except Antarctica and everywhere on those continents except for the most scorching deserts, the iciest places, and a few small, bat-free islands scattered around the world. About 47 species of bats live in North America north of Mexico.

Hanging Out

Straw-colored flying foxes (*Eidolon helvum*) roost in trees, looking like a load of wash that flew through soot, turned half black, and scattered. These big groups of flying foxes are called camps.

Batman, his bats, and many other bats roost in caves, but bats also call home old mines, buildings, and trees. Some fruit bats that live in the *tropics* make tents by biting through big leaves. The Hardwicke's lesser mouse-tailed bat even lives in the pyramids in Egypt.

A Cozy Tent

Honduran white bats (*Ectophylla alba*) make a tent in a leaf of a *Heliconia* tree, a relation of the banana tree. The bats chew along the leaf until the top part flops over. Sunlight coming through the leaf turns the bats pale green, hiding them. When the old leaf is worn out, the bats will make a new tent.

Bringing Up Baby Bats

Bracken Cave, in southern Texas, is home to 20 million Mexican free-tailed bats. This huge number of animals is the biggest bat *colony* in the world. In June of each year, after the Mexican freetail mothers have their babies, you'll find almost 40 million bats. The baby Mexican free-tailed bats are born about a fourth the size of the adult bats.

MOTHER AND BABY

Bats are mammals, so baby bats feed on their mother's milk after they are born, just like puppies, calves, and human babies.

BAT NURSERY
After a long night of hunting insects, Mexican free-tailed bats return to their roosts on the ceiling of the cave. Tiny, hairless pink baby bats are already clinging to the ceiling.

The hairless babies hang together as pink patches on the ceiling of the cave—the adult bats are in brown patches. Each mother bat finds her baby several times a day to nurse it, picking out her baby from the crowd by its smell and the sound of its cries. Since as many as 500 of the bat pups cover each square foot of the cave ceiling, it's quite impressive that the mother bat can find her own pup. If another baby bat tries to nurse, the mother won't let it and may whack it with her wing. Bats have baby teeth at first, like humans, and then get adult teeth.

The baby bats begin flapping their wings, getting ready to fly, when they are about three to four weeks old. The young bats in Bracken Cave must fly the first time they try it and not fall—far below, the cave floor is crawling with *carnivorous* (meat-eating) beetles. If a bat falls to the floor, the beetles eat it down to the bones in minutes. The baby bats are flying and beginning to feed themselves by the time they're just four to

Bat Food and How Bats Get It

Bats leave their roosts at different times during the evening. Because they are *nocturnal*, or awake at night, the bats get ready to fly at about sundown. No one knows how the bats decide exactly when to take off for the night—but they definitely have a long conversation about it. Under the Congress Avenue Bridge in Austin, Texas, each evening as the sun sets, you can hear the lively squeaking of a million or so bats making plans.

Bats That Eat Insects, Spiders, and Other Creepy Crawlies

The insect-eating bats, like the Mexican freetails at Carlsbad Caverns, Bracken Cave, and the Congress Avenue Bridge, zoom through the sky once they leave their home cave or bridge. Mexican free-tailed bats in a tailwind can blow by you at more than 60 miles per hour (97 kilometers per hour), and they can fly up to two miles (3.2 kilometers) high. Most bats do eat insects—70 percent of all bats, or seven out of 10.

DANGEROUS PREY

A pallid bat (*Antrozous pallidus*) catches a centipede. Pallid bats feed on animals that crawl on the ground: crickets, grasshoppers, spiders, and huge centipedes. Although scorpions and centipedes have powerful stings, the bats still eat them and are not harmed. The pallid bat mashes its prey on the ground to kill it and disarm its sting.

A hunting bat uses echolocation, or pulses of sound, to find insects to eat.

Even in complete darkness, bats find insects and other animals to eat by *echolocation*. The lumps, wrinkles, and ridges on the faces of insect-eating bats help them point outgoing sound waves and get echoes back from objects. The sound pulses are usually at too high a *frequency* for humans to hear. If the sound pulses hit an insect, they bounce back to the bat's ears. The bat can tell from the time it took the sound pulses to get back how far away the insect is. Also, the sound will be weaker when it comes back to the bat. That also gives the bat information about the insect's position and the direction it intends to go.

Bats can hunt only one insect at a time. The bat has to finish sending the sound pulses and then wait to receive them back—it doesn't send pulses at a lot of insects at once.

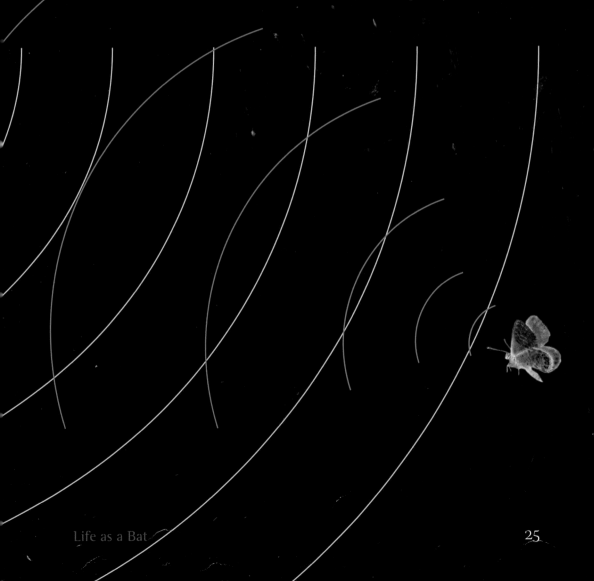

Bats also use echolocation to avoid obstacles. Echolocation works very well for bats, as anyone can tell you who has seen bats zigzagging through the evening sky, avoiding trees, telephone poles, and people. If you're wondering where you heard about echolocation before, dolphins and submarines also use it.

Sometimes the insects fight back. They can hear the bats' clicks, and the insects may take evasive action, going into a dive or just flying away. Tiger moths click right back at the bats to confuse them. But insect-eating bats usually catch a good meal.

Bats also use their ears for regular hearing and their voices to talk to other bats. When they are just talking and not hunting food, bats sometimes talk at a frequency that humans can hear.

What Bats Talk About

If bats could talk, they would have a lot to talk about—when to leave the bat cave for the evening, when to head south for the winter, who gets to be where on the cave ceiling. Somehow, bats do need to communicate. It turns out that they do. Bats use a mix of squeaks, chirps, and buzzes to say different things.

Barbara French, the science officer at Bat Conservation International (BCI), works at BCI headquarters in Austin, Texas, during the day. After her day job, she goes home to 50 to 75 roommates—Mexican free-tailed bats that were injured and can't go back into the wild. In her Bat Barn, the bats roost comfortably in blue denim pouches along the wall. The bats often talk to each other.

TAKING CARE OF ORPHANS
Barbara French gently checks Doc's heart and lungs with a neonatal stethoscope (a stethoscope for a newborn). The tiny Mexican freetail bat rests on a comfortable stuffed toy.

26

A Safe Home
Johnny, Molly, and Precious, a male and two female Mexican
freetails that French is caring for, peek out from their cloth roost.

When a million bats talk at once under the Congress Avenue Bridge in Austin, it's hard to tell what anyone is saying. But when one or two bats talk to each other in the Bat Barn, you can tune into their conversation. For more than 15 years, Barbara French and Amanda Lollar, at the Bat World Sanctuary in Mineral Wells, Texas, have studied their bats' talk. They record the calls and then see what behavior goes with a call. A bat might jump toward another bat, chittering and looking like it wants to play. The bat will say the same thing each time it's suggesting play.

Everyone knows that bats use sound to echolocate at night while they're hunting food. But it turns out that bats have conversations in the roost too. Bats greet each other, swap information, and argue. They use talk to attract a mate, warn a rival male away from their territory, or squabble over a favorite roosting spot. Barbara French and Amanda Lollar can understand about 20 different calls that their bats use.

Like people, bats may move the same sound, or word, around in a sentence to mean different things. "Chirp . . . chirp . . . chirp . . . buzz . . . buzz" might mean, "Stay away or there'll be trouble." "Chirp . . . chirp . . . chirp . . . trill . . . buzz . . . buzz" might mean, "You're pretty cute. You wanna come over to my place?"

Bat talk is causing scientists to think again about human talk. Until recently scientists thought that only humans had such complicated rules for speech.

Bat Talk

Here are a few Mexican free-tailed bat calls, with a rough human translation from Barbara French:

Alarm call: "Danger!"

Irritation buzz: "Stop it!"

Protest squeal: "Let go of me!"

Exaggerated chittering: "Move over."

Anticipation click: "I'm ready to eat."

Food solicitation buzz (bat to human): "Feed me!"

Herding buzz (male to females in his territory): "Cluster together, girls."

Territorial buzz (male to everyone): "This is my territory and all the girls inside belong to me."

Courtship song (male to females): "Hey, girls, look my way."

Warning call: "Get away from me!"

Directive call (mom to baby): "I'm coming. Where are you?"

Isolation call (baby to mom): "I'm hungry. Feed me!"

Bats That Eat Fruit, Nectar, and Pollen

Flying foxes and many other types of bats are plant eaters. These bats find their food by smell and use their eyesight to zero in on it. Flying foxes eat mostly fruit, but a few kinds drink or eat the nectar and pollen of flowers. Fruit-eating bats eat the fruit right where they find it on the plant or fly off with it to eat. As the bat flies, it spreads the fruit's seeds. A plant-eating bat can *pollinate* plants as it feeds on the nectar and pollen in one plant's flowers and then spreads those flowers' pollen to the next flowers the bat visits. A pollinated flower can then turn into fruit. More about how important bats are to *ecosystems* in chapter 5.

Bats That Eat Other Animals

Not all bats eat insects—some go for larger animals, like frogs, fish, or even other bats. The greater bulldog bat, found in Latin America, catches fish for food. The bat flies above quiet water, like a pool, and uses echolocation to detect a fish near the surface. The bat then drops low over the water, grabs the fish with the big claws on its feet, and flies off with the fish to eat it. The bat either eats the fish on the fly or stuffs it in its big cheek pouches and takes it to a good spot for eating, like a tree. Bulldog bats also eat insects.

The fringe-lipped bat (*Trachops cirrhosus*) eats frogs. Frogs croak loudly to find a partner but sometimes find a bat instead. Just from listening to a frog's croak, the bat can tell if the frog is poisonous or okay to eat. The bat dives at a tasty frog and grabs it with its teeth.

Vampire bats are another kind of bat that use other animals for food—vampires drink other animals' blood. More about them in chapter 4.

GOT ONE!
The greater bulldog bat
(*Noctilio leporinus*) can spear
fish up to three inches (eight
centimeters) long. Male bulldog bats
are red, and females are yellow.
This bat just had a good hunt
and speared a minnow
right out of the water.

Where Do Bats Go in the Winter?

When fall and colder weather come, the insects that many bats depend on for food begin to die off. These bats then either fly to a warmer place (*migrate*) or sleep the winter away (*hibernate*). In about October, Mexican free-tailed bats fly to Mexico to find insects. Bats can travel huge distances each night, sometimes hundreds of miles. The Mexican freetails return to the United States in about March. Bats almost always return home, to the cave or barn or wherever they were born.

How bats find their way home is something of a mystery—or miracle. One cue bats seem to use is the earth's magnetic field. Bats carry in their bodies a substance called magnetite, which is magnetic, or affected by a magnet's pull. The magnetite is pulled by the earth's magnetic field just the way bits of iron are pulled by a bar magnet. Dolphins, birds, and even humans also carry magnetite (although what humans are doing with it is anybody's guess).

Scientists found that if they change the magnetic field, bats will fly in the wrong direction. Richard Holland caught 10 big brown bats (*Eptesicus fuscus*) living in a barn to test the bats' reaction to a magnetic field shifted from the direction of the earth's. For five of the bats, he shifted the magnetic field 90 degrees clockwise, and for the other five, he shifted the field counterclockwise. The bats were in the new magnetic fields for 45 minutes before and after sunset, which is the time the bats take off from the barn for a night of insect hunting. The bats could see the setting sun. Holland put tiny radio transmitters on the bats (good for tracking bats over a short flight) and let them go.

Sure enough, the bats that had been in the wrong magnetic fields flew the wrong way. But five of the bats, or half, realized they had made a mistake. Those bats somehow fixed the mistake and flew home. The scientists had to go get the other five, using the transmitters to track them. So the earth's magnetic field is part of how bats navigate, but not the whole story.

Tracking where bats go when they migrate isn't easy—it's a big world, and bats can fly long and far. Bats are also small and secretive, so tracking a migrating bat isn't like finding a migrating elephant. Bat scientists tried attaching bands to bats' wings and then looking for the banded bats after the bats had moved for the season. That didn't work so well because even if the scientist found where the bats ended up (the big-world problem), bats roost in huge colonies—the scientist had to look for a couple of banded bats among hundreds, thousands, or millions of bats.

A better way to track bats is to catch some bats in a net, cut off a small piece of fur from each bat, and then analyze the chemicals in the bats' fur. Bat scientist

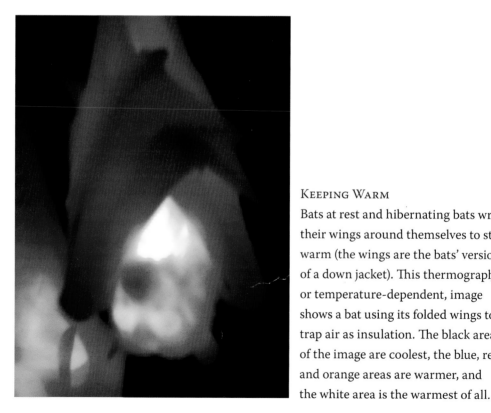

KEEPING WARM
Bats at rest and hibernating bats wrap their wings around themselves to stay warm (the wings are the bats' version of a down jacket). This thermographic, or temperature-dependent, image shows a bat using its folded wings to trap air as insulation. The black areas of the image are coolest, the blue, red, and orange areas are warmer, and the white area is the warmest of all.

BAT SLUMBER PARTY

Townsend's big-eared bats (*Corynorhinus townsendii*) cluster together for warmth as they hibernate. Their large ears will curl or straighten as the temperature changes, helping them control their body temperature, or thermoregulate.

Paul Cryan has done this for hoary bats. Hoary bats grow their winter coats while at their summer home, getting ready for the cold. Some of the chemicals (*isotopes*, or slightly different versions, of hydrogen) in the bat's coat will match the chemicals in the water the bat drank at its summer home. Those chemicals show how far south the bat was when it grew its coat. From this information, you don't know exactly where the bats were, but you have some idea. Hoary bats get around—they've been found in places as far apart as freezing Iceland and warm Bermuda. The studies on the bats' hair show that they may migrate from 250 miles (400 kilometers) to as far as 1,250 miles (2,000 kilometers) between their summer and their winter homes.

Other bats, like Townsend's big-eared bat, don't migrate and instead hibernate (the place where bats go to hibernate is called a hibernaculum). Bats that hibernate lower their body temperature to save energy. Mexican freetails can't hibernate, but some do stay in warm parts of the United States year-round.

In the Trees with Flying Foxes

A Scientist at 100 Feet Up

Scientists don't always stay in their laboratories, wearing white lab coats and mixing batches of chemicals. A scientist who wants to follow the bats sometimes has to climb trees—very high trees. And he might have to climb those trees in Ghana, Africa, and sleep in them on a small platform.

Bat scientist Dan Taylor's interest in flying foxes began when he realized how endangered they are. About 200 species of flying foxes in the Old World are vital to pollinating and spreading seeds in tropical forests. But these bats are actually sometimes eaten for food or farmers kill them, thinking they harm orchards.

Dan Taylor's platform he built in an iroko tree in Ghana, West Africa, to watch straw-colored flying foxes feed. Because the bats are nocturnal, or most active at night, he also had to sleep there.

One bat, the straw-colored flying fox, eats the fruit of the iroko tree, a valuable tree used as lumber. The fruit—which is something like a mulberry—makes up almost 90 percent of the straw-colored flying fox's food. A way to protect the bat would be to show officials in Africa that it is needed to spread iroko seeds, helping new trees to grow. Almost 17 percent of timber money in the country of Ghana, in western Africa, comes from the sale of iroko wood.

Near the city of Kumasi in Ghana is a colony of about 400,000 straw-colored flying foxes. The bats roost in treetops. Dan Taylor arranged with officials in Ghana to study the bats' feeding habits. But to study the bats, he had to go where they were—into the treetops. He and an assistant built three platforms 100 feet (30 meters) off the ground in iroko trees full of fruit.

To prove how important these flying foxes are to the iroko tree, Taylor set up experiments. He watched the bats with binoculars and other night vision equipment, recording which fruit-eating animals came to the trees, how much they ate, and whether they ate the seeds and passed them through or not.

Hanging with Bats

Taylor set seed traps on the ground at three points to measure the number of seeds dropped by bats or birds. At other places, he tested whether the seeds growing on the forest floor dropped by bats were eaten more or less often by insects than seeds dropped by a tree or other animals. In a third experiment, he put seeds put on damp paper in a shallow dish to see how the seeds did with no help from animals.

For four nights, only a couple of bats came to tree number 1, the biggest tree with the most fruit. The bats quietly made off with a couple of pieces of fruit and took them to a safe place to eat. On the fifth night, Taylor awoke to the calls of more than 250 straw-colored flying foxes around his platform. For three hours the bats crawled around the platform, eating fruit and spitting out seeds or flying off with fruit. All the while the bats had loud arguments and conversations. Suddenly, the bats were gone.

From their tree platforms, the scientists watched the bats for 30 days. In that time, the bats ate all the iroko fruit in those trees. Other animals, like monkeys and giant flying squirrels, ate the fruit too, but the seed traps showed that bats were the only animals spreading the seeds. From their results, Taylor could estimate that just one straw-colored flying fox, feeding around the nearby Kumasi zoo in Ghana, spreads an amazing 300 iroko seeds every night over hundreds or thousands of acres. The entire colony of bats spread more than 12 million seeds in just one night. The seeds spread by the bats also seemed to sprout faster and live longer than the seeds dropped by the trees. So flying foxes are vital to the iroko lumber business in Ghana.

The tiny shape on the iroko tree about halfway up, 80 feet (24 meters) in the air, is Dan Taylor, climbing.

OUT TO HUNT

A white-winged vampire bat
(*Diaemus yougi*) takes flight in
the evening, looking for prey.

CHAPTER FOUR

Attack of the Vampire Bats!

Real Vampires and the Full Moon

Even at night, the world isn't full of vampires. But vampires do exist—vampire bats, that is. There are three different species of vampire bats, although only one of those species lives completely on blood. The three species are the common vampire, *Desmodus rotundus* (which feeds on mammals); the white-winged vampire, *Diaemus youngi* (which feeds on mammals and birds); and the hairy-legged vampire, *Disphylla ecaudata* (which feeds only on birds). Vampire bats are found only in Latin America, the part of the world south of the United States that includes Mexico, Argentina, and other countries. The common vampire is best known to scientists, and so the following information is about common vampires. Most of it goes for the other two species of vampires too.

UP CLOSE
The fierce face of the
common vampire bat,
Desmodus rotundus.

TINY SKULL
The vampire's sharp incisors,
used to puncture the skin
of prey, show clearly in
this drawing of its skull.

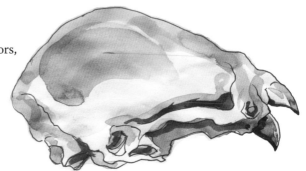

If you just look at a vampire bat, it's almost too scary to be true. Vampires have monster faces, with a squished-in snout and big pointed ears. Unlike other bats, common vampires are good runners—they use their long thumbs to pull themselves along the ground, and they often run up to their victim to feed. Vampires can also hop into the air from the ground. The vampires are small, only four inches (10 centimeters) long, and they weigh only two ounces (57 grams), but they really do have those vampire fangs, or incisors. Vampires aren't black—the common ones are gray-brown.

Hanging with Bats

Vampires may have evolved from fruit-eating bats. Or they could have gotten a taste for blood by eating blood-filled *parasites*, like ticks, which live on other animals' blood. They might have eaten insects that dig into other animals' skin, like screwworms, drinking the blood around the insects, and then evolved to drink only blood. Vampires have been on the planet for about six to eight million years. They are quite smart, with well-developed thinking areas of their brains. Planning to attack another animal takes intelligence.

Vampires Meet Columbus

Men sailing with Christopher Columbus were the first Europeans to see vampire bats, around the year 1500. They found the bats on the island of Trinidad, off the coast of the South American country Venezuela. In 1565, men with conquistador Hernán Cortés, who explored Latin America and the southwestern United States, described bats that bit people at night. Charles Darwin was the first scientist who saw a vampire bat (and maybe the first person anyone believed).

AN EARLY PORTRAIT
In 1838, Charles Darwin published this drawing of a vampire bat in *The Zoology of the Voyage of the H.M.S. Beagle.*

Attack of the Vampire Bats!

A Vampire Hunts Its Victim

Early in the night, the common vampire flies from its roost in a cave, tree hollow, or another spot to seek blood. It doesn't usually fly far, no more than three to five miles (five to eight kilometers). People are flaky about bats in general, but the strange habits of vampires get special attention. For example, most bats, including vampires, won't fly when the moon is full, as if they can't stand the light (just like you always thought!). Actually, the bats probably fly when the night is moonless and darkest to avoid *predators*.

Vampires can see and hear very well, and they use their eyes to spot an animal and their ears to listen for the animal's movements or breathing. They may also smell the animal or sense its body heat.

First the vampire licks a spot on its victim to soften up the skin. The vampire often picks a spot on the back or neck of a cow, where the blood supply is good right under the skin. The bat bites its victim with its sharp incisor teeth. These teeth are like a knife blade and make a wound about 0.2 inch (five millimeters) deep. The wound is crater shaped, like an asteroid hit on the moon.

The vampire has an anticoagulant in its saliva, made up of chemicals that keeps the blood flowing—the blood doesn't clot into a scab. If the blood clotted in a few minutes, the way it usually does when you get a cut, the bat would have to bite the animal again and again to feed. The vampire's bite isn't terribly painful, and usually the bitten animal doesn't even wake up. The vampire licks up the blood (it doesn't suck the life out of the animal). The blood moves through the bat's mouth in two channels under its tongue.

The common vampire may drink for as long as half an hour and will drink only two teaspoons of blood a night. That's half to all (50 to 100 percent) of the bat's weight. Other vampires often take the first vampire's place at the wound and feed.

High Jump

A common vampire (*Desmodus rotundus*) jumps, pushing off on its long thumbs. The vampire uses its thumbs to hop along or jump into the air to fly.

A Midnight Snack

Two white-winged vampires (*Diaemus youngi*) share a meal
of chicken blood. The vampires can drink so much blood
in a meal, they look like tennis balls. If a third vampire
tries to join the feast, the first two will try to fight it off.

Since the vampire needs the cow alive to feed on and doesn't want to turn the
cow into the walking dead, usually the vampire won't drain enough blood to hurt
its victim. Besides, the tiny real vampire doesn't need much blood. The cow is only
in trouble if a lot of vampires take a meal from it. A vampire must drink every two
nights or it will starve to death.

After a meal, the vampire flies off to a quiet place to digest it. Often, the bat
will return to the same animal the next night to feed again.

Vampires can actually be rather nice, at least to each other. A lucky vampire
that has found a meal of blood will sometimes share the blood with hungry vampires
back at the vampire roost. (The vampire that found the blood throws it up to feed
its friends—but no need to go into that.)

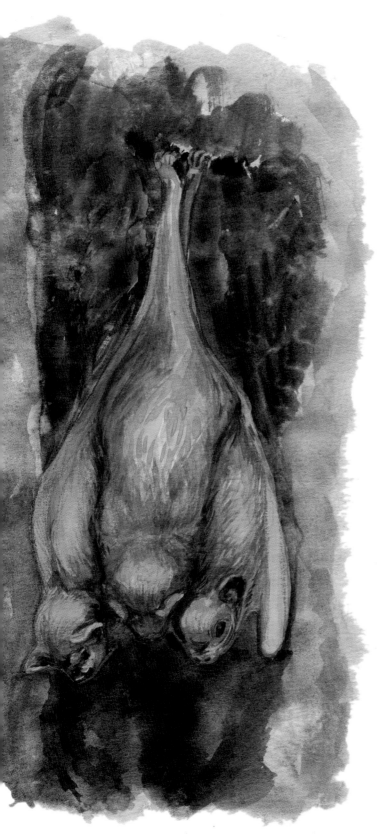

Vampires roost together and sometimes share food, but they hunt alone or in pairs.

What Would Happen If You Met a Vampire

Well, usually nothing—you've got an edge on a four-inch-tall animal. But if you're an angry rancher in Costa Rica whose cows just got bitten by a group of vampires, then the vampire would have a lot to fear. Another thing—most bats aren't vampires. Vampires make up one-third of 1 percent of all bats, which means that if you had 1,000 bats, collected from all over the world, a vampire probably wouldn't even be one of them. So you don't have a chance of meeting a vampire unless you travel to Latin America and go out in the dark. It's hard to say what you'd do if you saw one of those little vampires running along at high speed in the night.

Now and then, a vampire will bite a person. Then, even more terrifying, the vampire will come back, probably the next night, to feed again from that person. Worst of all, common vampire bats can tell people apart by the sound of their breathing. But to get rid of the vampire, all you have to do is shut your window at night. Bat vampires aren't supernatural, and even if you get bitten, you won't grow fangs yourself.

Attack of the Vampire Bats!

A white-winged vampire
(*Diaemus yougi*)

The Problem People Have with Real Vampires

A group of vampires can do damage—but usually only to cows, horses, and other farm or ranch animals. Of course, people probably caused the problem they have with the vampire bats, not the other way around. Years ago, vampires lived in forests, drinking the blood of wild big mammals like tapirs, pig-shaped animals with what looks like a short elephant's trunk. But farmers and ranchers cut down the forests to make fields for their crops and livestock, like cows. The juicy cows, all gathered, gave the bats an easy, big new food. More vampires are around now that they have so much good food.

The Bigger Problem Real Vampires Have with People

The problem for the rancher and the cow bitten by a vampire begins as the sun rises. The cow has an open cut on its skin. Now daytime pests move into the cut, like screwworms, a kind of fly that lays its eggs in a wound. The eggs hatch into *larvae*, which feed on the wound. It can become a long-term sore and infected.

The bite of vampire bats can give cows and other livestock rabies. Because the bats move from animal to animal to feed, they can spread the disease.

Ranchers with a vampire bat problem sometimes react violently against all bats. Vampires often roost with other kinds of bats. Usually about 20 vampires and their young roost together. Ranchers may destroy an entire cave full of thousands of bats—bats that eat insects, fruit, or nectar—just to kill a few vampires. If vampires are a serious pest to the ranchers (or the ranchers have become a serious pest to all bats and are killing huge numbers of them), the vampires can be caught in a net, painted with the chemical warfarin, and released. When the bat returns to its roost, other vampires will groom it and be poisoned by the warfarin.

A common vampire
(*Desmodus rotundus*)

44

A LOVER OF BLOOD Vlad the Impaler enjoys a picnic lunch while his henchmen stick hundreds of his enemies on stakes. This woodcut appeared in a German brochure printed in the 15th century.

Human Vampires

Vlad the Impaler (1431–1476) was the original human vampire. Even back in the 15th century, Vlad was called Count Dracula. *Dracula* means "son of the dragon," and Vlad was the ruler of Wallachia, in southern Romania. Vlad was a Crusader who fought to keep the Turks from the Ottoman Empire out of his country. At the time, the Ottoman Empire, based on the Muslim faith, threatened Romania, a Christian country. The real Vlad may not have drunk blood, but he certainly shed a lot of it. He fought many battles against the invading Turks, riding at the head of his army. He also killed huge numbers of Romanians, citizens of his own country, just to keep them terrified of him. Vlad sometimes murdered Romanians in clever ways. One time he fed a group of beggars at his castle. Then he had them burned to teach the rest of the people in his kingdom to earn their way and not to beg.

Because Vlad defended his country against its enemies, he is honored in Romania, not thought of as a nasty old vampire. More about Bram Stoker, the writer who turned Vlad into a vampire and a bat, in chapter six.

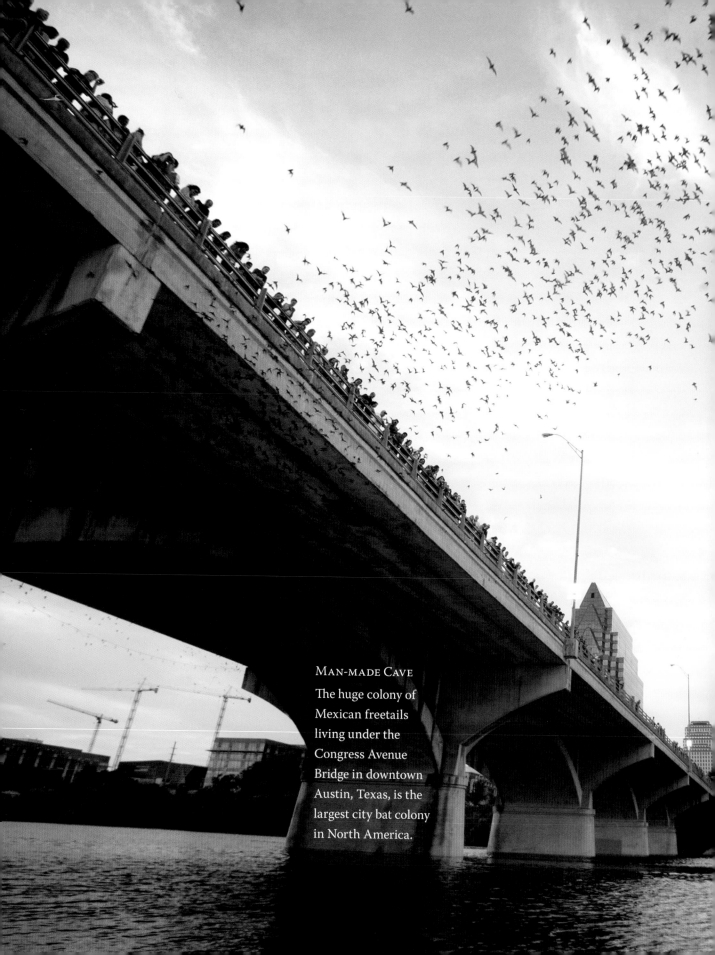

MAN-MADE CAVE
The huge colony of
Mexican freetails
living under the
Congress Avenue
Bridge in downtown
Austin, Texas, is the
largest city bat colony
in North America.

CHAPTER FIVE

In the Rain Forest or Under a Bridge

Bats' Worldwide Importance

The Ecology of Earth

Bats aren't just strange, darting shadows and a whisk of wings in the night. Like every plant and animal on earth, bats fit in. Bats are part of the earth's *biosphere*, which is made up of many different *ecosystems*. An ecosystem is a community of living *organisms* and their environment. Ecosystems can be large or small. For example, just the Mexican freetails and the other organisms in Carlsbad Caverns make up a small ecosystem. All the ecosystems on earth are joined in many ways, like by wind crossing from one ecosystem to another, by running water, and by the movements of animals.

THE WEB OF LIFE

A *food web* is a way of describing the movement of energy through an ecosystem. At the bottom of the food web are plants, which get energy from the sun. Animals eat the plants and get energy from them. Then other animals eat those animals and so on up to the top predator of the chain, which might be a snake or an owl. Because real-life food webs are so complicated and every part of the web affects every other part, it's hard to know what the effect of killing off just one animal will be. Once this is known, it may be too late to fix it.

Bats' Place in the World

Bats help ecosystems in several major ways: they eat insects, they pollinate plants, and they reseed forests. Most people have no idea how much work bats do. Each night in the summer, the 20 million Mexican free-tailed bats that live in Bracken Cave in Texas fly out of the cave and eat about 250 tons of insects. Yes, *every* night. Try to imagine a nice, warm summer night, sitting on the front steps of your house with a glass of lemonade—and having 250 more tons of insects joining you (a horse weighs about half a ton).

Bats eat, big-time, insects that destroy farmers' crops. According to Bat Conservation International, 150 big brown bats can eat enough cucumber beetles in one summer to save farmers a billion dollars a year. Those beetles, if they hadn't been eaten by bats, would have had 33 million larvae, or baby beetles, which are what attacks the crops. Just one insect-eating bat can eat 500 to 1,000 mosquito-size insects in an hour. Definitely the more bats in our lives, the better.

More than 100 species of bats live in the rain forests of South America. In the rain forest, bats pollinate many kinds of trees, like wild peach, banana, and mango trees. These trees need bats to pollinate them so that the trees can make fruit. The "tame," or cultivated, versions of these fruit trees, growing on farms, don't need bat pollination, but every so often the tame trees need to swap pollen with the wild ones to stay healthy. In the tropical forests of the Old World, more than 300 plant species need bats to pollinate them and spread their seeds. Probably many more plants that depend on bats will be discovered.

When rain forest trees are cut down for lumber, bats bring back the trees by dropping seeds as they fly over cleared areas. In some rain forests, bats start up to 98 percent of the first trees growing. Without bats, we would look out on a very different world.

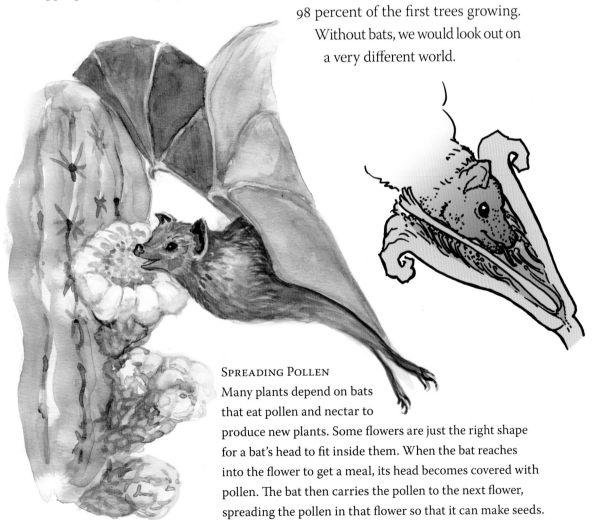

Spreading Pollen
Many plants depend on bats that eat pollen and nectar to produce new plants. Some flowers are just the right shape for a bat's head to fit inside them. When the bat reaches into the flower to get a meal, its head becomes covered with pollen. The bat then carries the pollen to the next flower, spreading the pollen in that flower so that it can make seeds.

For those people who don't react to bats by going, "Oh, what cute little guys!" bats have real money value. Bats first made money for people through the sale of guano, or bat droppings. That was the big money earner from bats when Jim White was poking around Carlsbad Caverns around the turn of the twentieth century.

Actually, all along bats were quietly helping people make money. Products made from plants pollinated or reseeded by bats are used in more than 450 important products, including food, drinks, and medicines.

Keeping Bats Alive

Natural Enemies of Bats—Birds of Prey and Snakes

Bats aren't at the very top of their food chain, and sometimes other animals eat them. Coach whip snakes sometimes hang over the opening to Bracken Cave and grab a bat or two out of the air as the bats leave the cave for the night. Because 20 million bats fly out of the cave each night, some bats have to get going while it's still light outside. A few are caught by red-tailed hawks, which are awake during the daytime. Owls, another animal flying at night, sometimes eat bats. Raccoons, skunks, and other mammals may get lucky and snag a bat coming out of a cave. But most of the bats escape each night.

UNLUCKY BAT

Snakes are one of bats' natural predators.

Hanging with Bats

Human Enemies of Bats—
Men with Dynamite and Poison

Bats are no match for humans bent on their destruction. A hawk or owl might now and then catch a bat, but a couple of people with dynamite, headed for a cave or mine where bats are roosting, can kill thousands of bats in one blow. Not long ago in Brazil, people dynamited or poisoned bats in more than 8,000 caves. These people seemed to be out to destroy not only bats, but a good portion of the planet. Humans sometimes go on a rampage against bats if a vampire bites a person. People still seem to be genuinely afraid of bats—or they have a strange sense of what's fun to do.

Bat *populations* may also go down when trees are cut either for sale as lumber or to make way for ranches and farms. Other bats may come under attack by fruit growers, who say the bats eat their bananas, mangoes, peaches, and other fruits. In fact, bats, like people, choose ripe fruits to eat—the fruit growers pick only green, or unripe, fruit to ship and sell.

Pesticides, like DDT (which stands for dichlorodiphenyltrichloroethane), can harm bats. DDT is great for whacking mosquitoes. This has to be a good thing since mosquitoes cause diseases that kill, like malaria, and mosquitoes are just nasty at picnics and everywhere else you can think of. The problem is, bats eat insects loaded with DDT and store it as fat for energy during migration. As the bats chemically break down the fat to use it as energy, large amounts of DDT are released into their bodies and can kill them. Mother bats may also pass DDT on to their young in milk, and the babies die of poison overload. Since bats usually have only one baby a year, they can't quickly recover from a poison disaster.

If we don't have bats for pest control, we'll have to step up the use of chemicals. Everyone knows that it can't be good to pile chemicals on our fruits, vegetables, and other food so that the insects don't eat it. DDT, here we come.

People Aren't All Bad When It Comes to Bats

People and bats often get along quite well once they have been properly introduced. Then people are usually happy to help *conserve* bats.

The Congress Avenue Bridge in Austin, Texas, is home to anywhere from 750,000 to 1.5 million Mexican free-tailed bats. The bats haven't lived under the bridge for long. In 1980, the city of Austin repaired the bridge. The repairs made narrow openings under the bridge, about 16 inches (40 centimeters) deep, that the bats found perfect to hang from. The bats come back to the bridge in the spring every year after spending the winter in Mexico.

At first, many people in Austin were afraid of the bats. The city newspaper ran alarming headlines. But 10 years later, the same paper called the bats "our furry friends." Austin celebrates Batfest every year, with bat watching, music, food, and displays. You can take a tour boat with a guide (and a bat symbol on the front of the boat) and go right under the Congress Avenue Bridge to see the bats.

Hanging with Bats

The people of Austin now love their bats, and droves
of tourists come to see them each year.

Close to sundown, the bats are getting ready to fly out from under the bridge
and eat 15 tons (13.5 metric tons) of corn earworm moths that are destroying the
cotton in nearby fields. The bats save the cotton—which will then be turned into
T-shirts, sheets, and other good stuff. They also bring in about $10 million a year
from the thousands of tourists who come to Austin to see them.

Bats often migrate from one country to another, and so all of the countries
the bats spend time in have to work together to help the bats. Mexican freetails are
one kind of bat that spends part of the year in one country, the warmer part in the
United States, and the other part of the year in another country, the colder part in
Mexico. For the first time, a conservation group in Mexico bought a bat cave, outside
Monterrey, to protect the bats living there. The bats had gone from a population of
about 20 million to 1.2 million.

What's annoying and hard to understand is that it's usually not hard to save
bats—people just don't do it. The golden rule ought to go for people and bats—"do
unto others as you would have others do unto you." A little knowledge about bats is
also useful if you want to help them.

Leave bats alone when they are in their roosts. In winter, a bat disturbed in
its roost might feel like you would if someone yanked off your blankets when you
were sleeping outside in the dead of winter. You might freeze to death. When bats
are hibernating in the winter, they cool down their body temperature almost to the
temperature of the air around them. Bats don't go into a deep sleep like bears and
are easy to rouse, or wake up. If the bats are disturbed and wake up, they may waste
as much as 30 days of energy. Since insects are dead in the winter, the bats have no
way to eat and get more energy. They really could die. In summer, females and their
babies must be left in peace in their roosts.

PEOPLE-FREE ZONE
This gate over the
old Nancy mine in
Socorro, New Mexico,
lets bats in and out but
keeps people away.

Another good way to help bats is to put the right kind of gate over an old mine. When a mine is no longer being used, the hole remains. Gates are sometimes put up to protect people from going in the dangerous old mine. But if bats are inside, they could be trapped. The answer is a bat-friendly gate, built so that bats can fly in and out. Bat Conservation International is working with the US Bureau of Land Management on building those gates—so far, they've built more than 1,000 gates. Many other groups are putting up gates too.

Hanging with Bats

Dipping for a Sip

Not all bats can swim well. Townsend's big-eared bat (*Corynorninus townsendii*) gets wet easily and could sink, so the bat stays higher over the water when drinking and laps the water up with its tongue.

Bats also need to drink a lot of water each day, as much as 50 percent of their weight. These days, many bats get water from livestock troughs. Since bats drink on the fly, swooping down to the water to drink and then flying away, anything that blocks the flyway might knock the bats out of the air. They can drown if the blow is so hard that they become unconscious or if they can't find a way out of the tank.

The answer is to have a big enough water source and build an escape ramp so that bats falling in the water can climb back out. Some bat species can drink out of a water source as small as three feet by four feet (0.9 by 1.2 meters), and Townsend's big-eared bat can drink out of a teacup. Most bats, though, need a stretch of water at least 10 feet long by 2.5 feet wide (3.1 by 0.8 meters). Some bats need even more than that. Bat Conservation International published a handbook for ranchers explaining how to help bats when building a livestock water trough.

Wind Power versus Bats

These days, everyone is worried about how to get clean energy. Many energy sources, like coal and oil, cause air and water pollution. Power plants can release gases, like carbon dioxide (CO_2), that trap heat and cause *global warming*. A cleaner environment would be good for people, bats, and all the other animals on earth.

Wind energy is an excellent way to get power to run electric lights, air conditioners, hair dryers, and thousands of other devices in houses, schools, and businesses. As a result, more and more wind turbines are springing up across the United States and around the world. The downside of wind power is that you get it by the blades of big turbines turning in the wind, and bats and birds can be hit by those fast-moving blades.

The number of dead bats found under turbines is frightening. For example, in just six weeks, 44 wind turbines in West Virginia killed between 1,364 and 1,980 bats. This problem with wind power caught bat experts by surprise. But *all* wind energy sites studied in North America and Europe have dead bats under them.

Hanging with Bats

No Source of Power to Flying Animals
Wind power turbines stretch across the land.
Wind power has great promise to supply clean
energy but may be deadly to bats and birds.

Bats are usually very good at avoiding crashes. One clue as to why bats run into wind turbines is that migratory bats are killed the most and are killed during the time when they are migrating. Migrating bats probably travel along routes where winds are high—which is just where you find wind turbines. Another clue is that the blades of wind turbines move very fast, at more than 150 miles per hour (242 kilometers per hour), much faster than a bat can fly—bats might not be able to get out of the way of those blades. At times, bats may be attracted to insects around the turbines. Bats could be attracted to the wind turbines themselves by the sight of them or sounds coming from them. For example, some bats that live in trees, like red bats and silver-haired bats, may mistake the wind turbines for big trees.

Wind turbines are a new source of power, so no one knows for sure why bats seem to be attracted to them. Since the wind power industry predicts that in a few years, wind power will increase by 150 percent, the wind-power-versus-bats problem has to be solved.

Bat Conservation International, as the group so often does, is helping to save bats, this time from the blades of wind turbines. BCI formed the Bats and Wind Energy Cooperative (BWEC) in 2003, with the US Fish and Wildlife Service, the American Wind Energy Association, and the National Renewable Energy Laboratory of the US Department of Energy. The BWEC group looks for wind energy sites that won't harm bats or other wildlife. Detectors as tall as wind turbines (144 feet, or 44 meters) listen to bats, gathering information on what bats are doing at wind turbine sites before the turbines are built. Scientists are also working on sending signals that the bats can hear from the turbines so that the bats stay clear. Some power companies are helping by allowing the studies to take place where their wind turbines are. Other companies aren't so environment friendly after all—the bat scientists aren't allowed on their property.

A Tiny Transmitter

The radio transmitters that are attached to bats must be tiny so that the bat can still fly while carrying the load, but then the batteries don't last very long.

Counting Bats

Sometimes, with all the goodwill in the world, it's hard to help bats—how do you know which bats need help and where? Counting bats one year and then seeing if more or fewer bats are around the next year isn't easy. Bats usually fly at night and often roost in hidden, out-of-the-way places. Or they gather in places that make it difficult for people to reach them, like the treetops of Ghana. Accurate counts of bat populations are important, especially if a species is endangered.

Large animals like whales or birds can be tracked by fastening a battery-powered device to them. Tundra swans migrate 10,000 miles (16,100 kilometers) round-trip from the Atlantic Ocean coast to the Canadian Arctic and back. A battery weighing three ounces (85 grams) is harnessed to a swan, and a satellite follows the swan's long migration. Tundra swans weigh from 10 to 20 pounds (4.5 to nine kilograms), and so carrying a three-ounce battery while flying is no problem for them. Mexican freetails weigh less than half an ounce, and so a giant three-ounce battery can't be fastened to them. Tiny batteries can be put on bats, but the batteries quickly run out of power.

You can count bats by walking into a cave where they're roosting, looking up at the ceiling, and guessing how many bats cover a square foot (a square foot is a square that is 12 inches on each side). Then you can multiply the number of bats in a square foot times the number of square feet the bats are covering in the cave. But this doesn't give an accurate number—the inside of caves is dark. Besides, tromping around the cave disturbs the bats.

Another way to count bats is to take a flash camera picture of them as they come out of a cave in the evening. Then you count the number of bats in the picture and multiply that number by how long it takes all the bats to fly out of the cave. This number isn't accurate either—bats may fly back into the cave, and other species of bats may live in the cave. Camera flashes also disturb bats.

A camera that picks up temperature change can be used to count bats. Biologists Thomas Kunz, Loren Ammerman, and Nickolay Hristov used infrared thermal imaging to count Mexican long-nosed bats from a cave in Big Bend National Park, in west Texas. The bats spend summers at the cave and winters in Mexico. Mexican long-nosed bats are endangered and only live in Texas and New Mexico. They feed on nectar and are key pollinators of agave and cactus plants.

With the infrared camera, as the bats come out of the cave at night, they show up as warm spots against the cooler air. Different species of bats show up as different shapes in the camera. The bats in the infrared images still have to be counted. Using infrared cameras to record bat numbers is more expensive and takes longer than the usual ways, but infrared is more accurate.

Extinction

When Plants and Animals Are Gone for Good

Extinction is a negative word—it's when your campfire goes out or it's when a species, or kind of animal or plant, dies out, never to be seen again. But although extinction sounds terrible, for millions of years, it has been the way of life. Dinosaurs are extinct, probably killed by global cooling when a huge meteor slammed into the earth. The impact caused a heavy fog to blanket the earth for many years and block the sun. Global warming and cooling have happened many times before, and lots of animals and plants couldn't survive in the new, hotter or cooler environment.

On the one hand, extinction is a natural process. On the other hand, humans shouldn't kill off every other species of animal or plant except beef cows and corn just because we think we're the most important animals on the planet. We'll be sorry if we do—so many other animals and plants serve a purpose, even if it's not obvious. Plants may seem to be just hanging out, nodding in the sun or dripping in the rain, but without them, humans couldn't breathe—plants make the oxygen that we need to survive.

In 1973, the federal government passed the Endangered Species Act to protect plants and animals that were in danger of dying off. At that time, bald eagles, the national symbol of the United States, were endangered. The pesticide DDT was the culprit in killing the eagles, just as it was for bats. DDT washed into streams and then got into plants and animals in the streams, including fish. The eagles ate the fish with the DDT. It made the shells of the eagles' eggs so thin that they broke, and the baby eagles died before they ever hatched. Now DDT can't be used in the United States.

The great news about the bald eagles is that they're back. The US Fish and Wildlife Service, the government agency that watches over species of animals and plants in the United States, recently took eagles off the list of threatened or endangered species. (*Endangered* means a species is thought to be in danger of extinction. *Threatened* means a species is likely to become endangered but isn't in danger of extinction.) Now bald eagles fill the skies again.

Many species of bats are endangered or threatened—about half of the 47 species in North America are endangered or decreasing in numbers fast. On other continents, some species of the lovely flying foxes are already extinct.

GONE FOR GOOD

These animals are all extinct, but some died out because of natural climate change and other changes in their environment, and some died out because of human actions. The passenger pigeon and dodo both became extinct in the last 100 years because humans killed too many of them.

TYRANNOSAUROUS REX

ARCHAEOPTERYX

WOOLLY
MAMMOTH

SABERTOOTH
CAT

QUAGGA

DODO

PASSENGER
PIGEON

It's hard to say how endangered or threatened a lot of bat species are. But humans need bats in every possible way that we could need another animal. Bats give us food through their pollination of plants and reseeding of forests, and they control the pest insects that would eat that food. Could we really live without them?

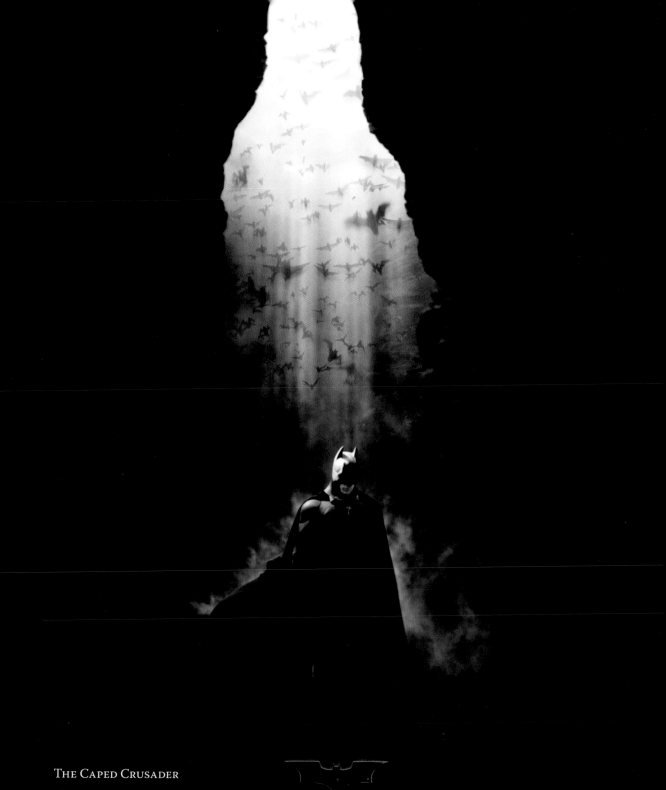

THE CAPED CRUSADER

The movie *Batman Begins* shows bats
on the side of good, but does anyone
really think of Batman as a bat?
And that bat signal in the sky—the
echolocation of real bats is way cooler.

CHAPTER SIX

Bats on the Big Screen and Other Imaginary Bats

Major and Minor Bat Myths

*It's Better to Know the Truth about Something
If You're Going to Spend a Lot of Time Being Afraid of It*

Bat Tales

What is really strange is that people dreamed up vampires before they found real ones. People were certain that the dead returned to drink the blood of the living long before explorers of the New World found vampire bats.

Before Thomas Edison and electricity on every street corner, the nights were dark, silent, and dangerous, lit only by candles and lanterns. In Europe, wolves howled in the night, and it could be dangerous to go outside. People could die of the slightest cut or illness—even young adults, children, and babies. The causes of disease, like bacteria and viruses, weren't known, and modern medicines, like antibiotics, didn't exist. So people who feared the night weren't just foolish and superstitious—they had to be careful.

Even the ancient Greeks and Romans had stories about bats behaving badly. In 600 BC, the Greek Aesop told a fable about a bat that borrowed money to start a business. The business failed, and so the bat had to hide during the day to avoid the people it owed money to. That, Aesop said, was the beginning of bats coming out just at night.

It's odd, but the small bats are the ones everyone fears. People are suspicious of the little bats that hide away in caves and other dark places and are seen only at night.

The big flying foxes, which live right out in the open in trees, are considered signs of good luck in many countries, like China. Over the centuries, bats have appeared in Chinese art—sculptors made beautiful bats out of jade and ivory. In the emperor's Summer Palace, in Beijing, large numbers of colorful bats are painted on the ceiling.

The Chinese word for *bat* is even said in the same way as the word for *happiness.* The ancient Chinese symbol *wu-fu* is made up of five bats, which stand for the five happinesses of China— health, wealth, long life, good luck, and tranquility. The five bats circle the symbol for prosperity.

In the Fiji islands of the South Pacific Ocean, rats, not bats, are said to have had the first wings— flying foxes walked. One day, a flying fox borrowed a rat's wings and wouldn't give them back. Now rats eat baby bats to get even, and so flying foxes don't leave their babies by themselves.

GOLDEN BAT
The Chinese show their appreciation of bats with this design of a bat at a Buddhist shrine.

INDIAN TALES
Many native cultures honor bats. In this illustration of a Native American folktale by Charles Livingston Bull, the bat joins the birds in a ball game.

In some places in India, the Indian flying fox (*Pteropus giganteus*) is sacred. This is a huge bat, with a wingspan of four to five feet (1.2 to 1.5 meters). The Indian flying fox eats figs, mangoes, and other fruits and spreads the seeds. According to a Bat Conservation International report, in the Indian village of Puliangulam, in southern India, a colony of about 500 Indian flying foxes is thought to be sacred. The bats roost in one big banyan tree and have been there for decades.

The villagers in Puliangulam say that the bats are protected by a god named Muni, who lives around the bats' tree. The villagers must protect the bats. If a villager harms them, he or she will be punished—even by the death of a family member. To be forgiven, the villager who harmed the bat must do a ceremony for Muni.

In Western literature, the bat is often
portrayed as a fearful beast. In this
nineteenth-century illustration by
Elizabeth Shippen Green, the bat is one
of the creatures that haunt the night.

But in other parts of India, bats are killed for food or medicine. The Indian
government puts flying foxes in the same category, "vermin," as rats and poisonous
snakes—and bats can get the same treatment.

A favorite bat legend is that bats get stuck in your hair. Bats are such excellent
flyers, it's hard to believe they could run into a head of hair—with echolocating, they
can detect just one human hair in the dark. How could a bat crash into 100,000
hairs, the average number on one human head?

But somehow, SOMEHOW, the bat-in-the-hair story got started, so maybe once
a bat did invade somebody's hair. A young bat could have been trapped in somebody's
house. As the bat, not such a good flyer yet, frantically searched for a way outside,
it might have flown into a puffy hairdo. Bats sometimes fly close to people's hair,
probably looking for insects, and somebody may have imagined just how awful it
would be if the bat got stuck. Even if a bat did get in your hair, it wouldn't be the worst
thing that ever happened to you—there's no way the bat would pull it all out.

Bat Diseases

Here's the truth about a human getting sick from a bat. Yes, bats can give two
diseases to humans. One disease, histoplasmosis, is rare and caused by a fungus.
People who get histoplasmosis spend a lot of time breathing in the dust from bat or
bird guano, which is where the fungus lives. Jim White, the discoverer of Carlsbad
Caverns, probably should have worried about getting histoplasmosis—in his day,
the caves held tons of bat guano. But he didn't, and he doesn't seem to have gotten
it. You probably don't have to worry about it either unless you spend a lot of time in
bat caves. Sometimes people who do wear a respirator, a mask that filters air.

SO HAUNTED AT MOONLIGHT WITH BAT AND OWL AND GHOSTLY MOTH —

Bats on the Big Screen and Other Imaginary Bats

The other disease bats can give to humans is rabies. Rabies can kill a person. The disease is caused by a virus, and all mammals can get it. It's passed on through saliva, or spit, and so a rabid animal's bite can cause it. The Centers for Disease Control and Prevention, the government group that studies and watches out for diseases in the United States, points out that you can't get rabies just from looking at a bat in an attic, in a cave, or in the sky. For years the people of Austin, Texas, have been looking at the huge number of bats under the Congress Avenue Bridge, and nobody has died from it yet.

Many kinds of wild animal can get sick with rabies—like skunks, raccoons, and foxes. That's one reason you're not supposed to touch any wild animal. And a wild animal that doesn't run from you and will let you touch it is more likely to be sick. Vampires are the only bats that cause real outbreaks of rabies, mostly in farm animals like cows. They drink the blood of the animals and pass on the disease that way.

The truth is, the chance of you dying from a disease from a bat is way less than one in a million—you have a much better chance of falling in the bathtub and dying. So maybe you should keep an eye on that evil bathtub and not worry too much about bats. And if you see a sick bat or a sick skunk, raccoon, or fox, absolutely do not go close to it or grab it with your bare hands. (As if you would.) The odds of anyone dying of rabies from a bat are fewer than one person in 100 million. Only one or two people get rabies from any animal each year in the United States.

Hanging with Bats

Bats aren't filthy little beasts, whatever you may have heard (neither are rats, actually). They spend a lot of time grooming their fur and look clean and healthy. Orphaned bats can bond with humans and will even introduce their pups to their people.

People sometimes react in crazy ways when they find bats living in their houses, but really there's nothing scary about sharing your house with bats. The only problem is having hundreds of wild animals in the house that aren't toilet trained. . . . You get the picture.

If just one bat gets in your house, it's probably a young bat that didn't know any better. First of all, don't freak out—the bat is probably much more terrified than you are, and it won't hurt you. To get rid of the bat, you can do one of two things: call animal control or carefully deal with the bat yourself. Try closing the doors that lead to other rooms and opening windows and doors to the outside so that the bat can leave. You can also catch the bat with a net, but then you've got to be very careful handling it. The scared bat may bite when it's picked up, so get an adult involved who is wearing thick gloves. Another way to get rid of the bat is to wait for it to land on a flat surface, like a wall, and then cover it with a box. Then you can push a piece of cardboard between the box and the wall and take your box with the bat outside to release it.

Whatever you do, don't blast a bat with poison. That's a rotten thing to do (how would you like a faceful of Raid?), and guess what—the poison will slam you too. If a big group of bats is living in your house, you'll need expert help to get them out. One way to get a bunch of bats out of your house is to build them their own house (see chapter 7 and the If You Want to Know More section for help with moving bats). As Merlin Tuttle, the founder of Bat Conservation International, says, you don't have to declare war on bats. You can all live together in peace.

Weird Sayings about Bats

So how did people come up with the expression "blind as a bat"? Bats see as well as other mammals, and some kinds of bat, like vampires, have good sight. Bats can also see at night, just not in color. The only time a bat may seem to be blind is when it's trapped in a house. As the bat struggles to fly in the small area of a room, it may bump "blindly" into walls. A hundred years ago, E. Cobham Brewer wrote in his book *Dictionary of Phrase and Fable*, "A bat is not blind, but when it enters a room well lighted, it cannot see, and blunders about."

"Bats in your belfry" is another bat phrase. The usual meaning of the word *belfry* is "bell tower," and a bell tower is usually on top of a church. When you have bats in your belfry, the "belfry" is of course your head. Basically, you're acting silly, like you have bats flapping around in your head. This phrase might sound old and British, but actually an American author, George W. Peck, came up with it in his book *Peck's Uncle Ike and the Red-Headed Boy*, published in 1901: "They all thought a crazy man with bats in his belfry had got loose."

Belfries aren't found on churches so much anymore, and now people just refer to someone as "bats" ("You're bats!") or "batty" ("my batty aunt Martha"). "Batty" is also an American saying. In 1903, in his book *Slang Fables from Afar*, Al Kleberg wrote, "She . . . acted so queer . . . that he decided she was Batty."

Hollywood Bats

When movies got going in the twentieth century, bats became movie stars right along with people. At first, though, bats didn't get any fame or fortune. Or if they got fame, it was the wrong kind.

The word *vampire* comes from the old *Slavic* word *vampir*, meaning "blood drunkenness." The vampire myths from Eastern Europe, including Romania, first put forward the idea that a vampire could travel as an animal or smoke. But the real vampire bats were only in Latin America, and bats hadn't turned into human-size vampires yet.

Bram Stoker, who wrote the book *Dracula* in 1897, combined the discovery of vampire bats in the New World with Vlad the Impaler stories to create Count Dracula, the most frightening human vampire of all time. Soon after, Hollywood jumped on board with a whole string of Dracula movies.

A BEST SELLER

Bram Stoker's *Dracula* was first published in 1897 and has never been out of print. It's one of the most popular scary stories ever written.

BEFORE COUNT DRACULA . . .

In 1922, the very first human vampire movie, called *Nosferatu*, came to German movie theaters. Actor Max Schreck starred as the horrible Count Orlock. (The actor's last name even means "fright" in German. *Nosferatu* is an invented Romanian word for "vampire.") This vampire looks more like a rat than a bat.

The Romanian actor Bela Lugosi played a vampire in the 1931 movie *Dracula*. Bela Lugosi invented the classic vampire look with the black eyebrows, flowing cape, and diabolical laugh. (Eddie Munster borrowed that eyebrow look in the old TV series *The Munsters*.)

In the 1941 movie *The Devil Bat*, Lugosi played a mad scientist with an even madder killer bat. "Yes, you will strike. To kill," Lugosi says to his huge, fake-looking bat while they're alone in his secret laboratory. The bat goes out and slits the throats of a bunch of people wearing a certain kind of aftershave.

The TV series *Batman* came along in 1966. Batman had pointed ears and a cape that looked like wings, but no bat ever wore tights or gave a lecture about good behavior at the end of each show. The TV show probably didn't do much plus or minus for bats.

Bats' image got a bit of a boost from the Batman movies—*Batman* (1989), *Batman Returns* (1992), *Batman Forever* (1995), *Batman and Robin* (1997), and *Batman Begins* (2005). The movies were more worth watching than the TV show in a lot of ways (better costumes, better actors, better special effects). *Batman Begins* is the most serious, least cartoony of the Batman movies. Here we learn that as a child, Bruce Wayne was attacked by bats when he fell into a deep hole. The problem is, bats don't attack people. But as an adult and a "bat," Bruce Wayne does exactly this.

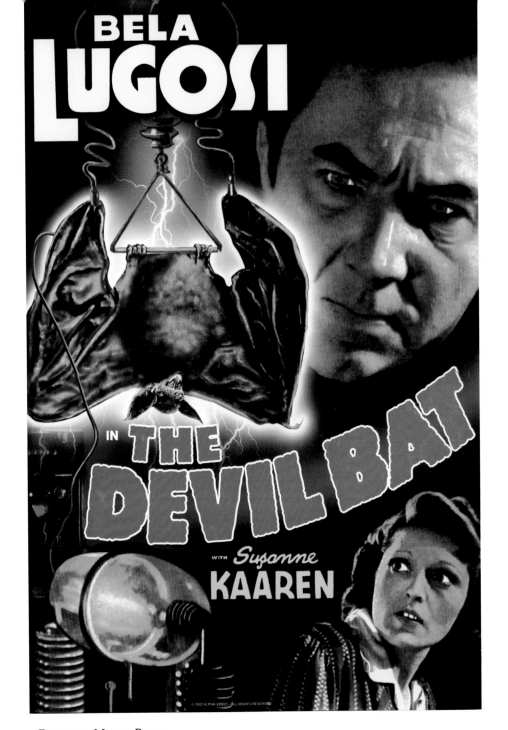

Fiendish Movie Bats

In the movie *The Devil Bat*, Bela Lugosi, playing the evil scientist
Dr. Paul Carruthers, gives orders to the monster bat he has created.
The bat, which looks like a stuffed flying fox, goes out every night
and kills people for revenge. The bat turned evil when it was zapped
with electricity.

Bats on the Big Screen and Other Imaginary Bats

"Why bats, sir?" asks Alfred, Bruce's butler. "Bats frighten me. It's time my enemies share my dread," Bruce replies.

So *Batman Begins* really has the same message as earlier bat movies—bats are to be feared and bats try to kill people. Even though Batman is a good guy, he's not entirely sane. After you've seen the movies, you probably wouldn't want him or a real bat flapping at you in your attic.

The 1999 movie *Bats*, starring Lou Diamond Phillips, is really just a remake of *The Devil Bat*—same evil scientist, same evil bats. (Scientists also have an image problem in movies.) This time, the bats became monsters when a scientist at a laboratory secretly infected Indonesian flying foxes with a virus. Once again, the bats go out and slit human throats—then they tear their victims to pieces. The government appears to be involved in a cover-up.

Human vampires turn from evil to good in the 1992 movie *Dracula*, where the old Dracula monster from Romania can still feel love. In this movie, a vampire bat appears on-screen, but it's not exactly a star performance. Dr. Van Helsing, who kills many human vampires in the movie, first appears giving medical students a lecture on blood. "Cute little vermin," the doctor says, holding up the vampire bat—which promptly bites him. After this, bats appear only as shadows in the movie. Dracula is said to control bats (and rats and wolves). In the end, he does turn good, but only after he stops being a vampire—and a bat.

Not long ago, bats rated a spot on a TV show called *Monster Myths*, on the Animal Planet channel. Vampire bats got listed as the third-most-feared monster in the world, right after wolves and gorillas and just ahead of piranhas. The show did try to explode vampire myths. For example, since vampires have to drink as much as their own weight in blood every day, a human vampire like Dracula would have to drink the blood of a whole table full of guests every night just to keep going. That seems unlikely.

One of the most accurate movies about bats is the comedy *Black Sheep*, starring Chris Farley and David Spade. In the movie, Mike (Chris Farley) and Steve (David Spade) find themselves spending the night in a cabin in the woods. This is Mike's punishment for royally screwing up his brother's campaign to be governor. Of course, part of the ultimate punishment is running into a bat.

The bat in *Black Sheep* is pretty real looking, as movie bats go. And the humans' terror when they see a bat seems right on. "I HATE bats!" Mike yells. The "bat" swoops at him. "I'M GONNA GET RABIES!" Mike yells, trying to squeeze under the bed. Mike and Steve chase the bat around the cabin with a broom, a frying pan, and a sheet stretched between them. At last the sheet works to get rid of the bat—Mike and Steve dump it outside. The two realize they've been idiots and pretend nothing happened. "Good night, Steve," Mike says. "Good night, Mike," says Steve.

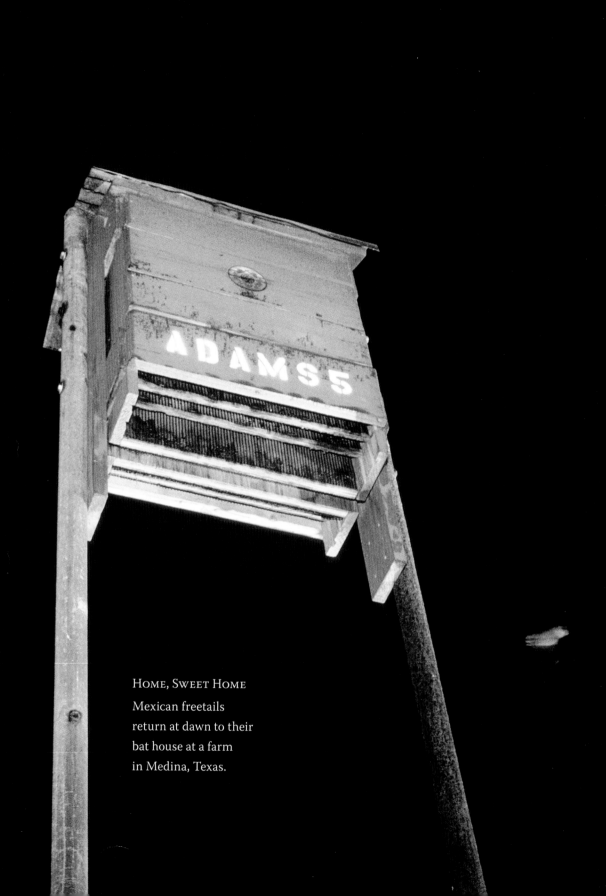

HOME, SWEET HOME
Mexican freetails
return at dawn to their
bat house at a farm
in Medina, Texas.

CHAPTER SEVEN

Building a Bat Cave

Bringing Bats Home

One of the best ways to help bats is to build them a house. The number of bats in the world is decreasing, and a big reason for this is that people are cutting down big trees and destroying other natural bat roosts. So you might have a great insect population in your yard for bats to eat, but if the bats don't have anywhere nearby to live, you'll be getting rid of those insects with your flyswatter. Or the bats may move into your house. Hey, you cut down theirs. But if you build the bats their own house and plug up the holes where they're getting into your house—this has to be done by an expert so that the bats aren't trapped inside and starved to death—the bats often will move into their new home.

Since bats roost close together, just one house can give a hundred or more bats a place to live. Bats are found in so many areas of the country, chances are, you have some bats roosting near your house already. The bat houses described here are for insect-eating bats.

Building a Bat House from a Kit

The easiest way to build a bat house is to buy a kit from the Organization for Bat Conservation (OBC) or Bat Conservation International (BCI). You can order the kit online or call up OBC or BCI. Within days, a handsome bat house kit will arrive in a box. The kit from OBC has a flashy design of a bat on the front. When you open the box, you might say, "Oh, cool!" The wood of the pieces for the house is nicely sanded and finished, and you can imagine the bats liking it too.

The kits from either OBC or BCI have only seven pieces to put together and come with a set of directions and a bag of screws. For the final step of building the house, you'll have to go to the hardware store to buy a long pole to set the house on and caulk and wood glue to make the house weatherproof. This can be the part of the project where you feel like a real builder as you walk up and down the aisles of the hardware store, finding the right pole, glue, and other supplies. Unless the bat-friendly adult who is helping you build the bat house owns a power drill (and isn't afraid to use it), you might want to ask at the hardware store if someone will drill holes in your pole and bolt the bat house to it.

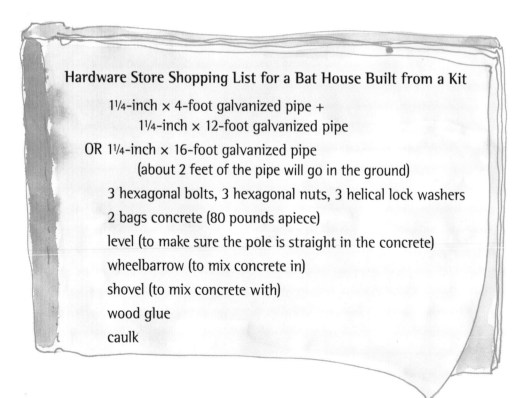

Hardware Store Shopping List for a Bat House Built from a Kit

1¼-inch × 4-foot galvanized pipe +
1¼-inch × 12-foot galvanized pipe

OR 1¼-inch × 16-foot galvanized pipe
(about 2 feet of the pipe will go in the ground)

3 hexagonal bolts, 3 hexagonal nuts, 3 helical lock washers

2 bags concrete (80 pounds apiece)

level (to make sure the pole is straight in the concrete)

wheelbarrow (to mix concrete in)

shovel (to mix concrete with)

wood glue

caulk

Jacky and Dave stand beside a bat house they helped build from a kit, ordered online from the Organization for Bat Conservation. In March, when the bats come back from their winter in Mexico, the house will be ready for them. In New Mexico, where Jacky and Dave live, the bats will stay in the house from March to October and then take off for Mexico again.

Make sure you have a long enough pole holding up your bat house, one that squirrels, cats, and other climbing animals can't get up. The pole should be metal and at least 12 feet (3.7 meters) high so that the bats feel safe. Mounting the pole in your garden or yard can be a bit tricky. It's best to set the pole in concrete so that the house doesn't sway in the wind. Bags of concrete can weigh about 80 pounds (36 kilograms), and the lime in concrete can burn your hands, so you don't want to touch it. This is another part of building a bat house where you'll need an adult friend to help you. Also, lifting the finished bat house, screwed to its metal pole, and setting it upright is a job for the strong.

The house from OBC isn't just pretty. The nylon mesh inside the house is just right for the bats to hold on to it with their toenails and hang upside down. Bats come in for a landing at their house like airplanes on a runway, and both the BCI and OBC houses have a carefully made landing area at the bottom of the house. They also have a slanted roof so that rain will run off and an opening for air.

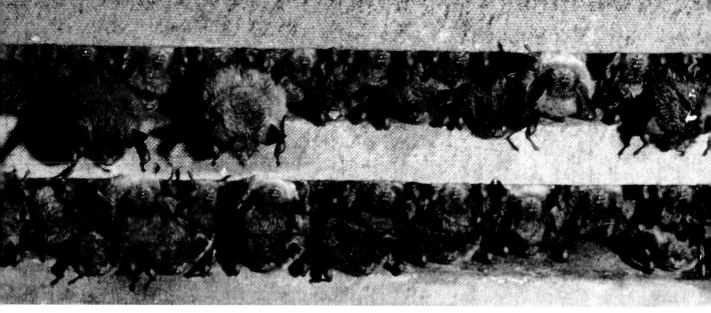

The color of a bat's house has to be right—lighter colors will make the house cooler than darker ones. Bats like a warm house, and so the house should be put in the sun, turned to the south or southeast to catch morning rays. In colder parts of the country, the house should be painted black to help warm it up. In the Southwest or South, where it's hot, paint your bat house a light color to reflect some of that heat away from the house. Paint also prevents the house from warping and keeps out rain. (Be sure to use a paint that won't poison the bats—see the instructions in your kit or plans.)

The spot where you put the house also has to be right. As the bats fly up to the house, they need airspace to slow and then land. The bat house shouldn't be too close to your house, trees, and or anything that blocks the bats' runway in the air.

Building a Bat House from Scratch

The somewhat harder way to build a bat house is from a set of plans, and you find the wood for the house and all the other materials. The plans to build some bat houses are also available from OBC and BCI—some of them are free online! (See the If You Want to Know More section for how to find the plans.) Probably you should not try to build a bat house just from a set of plans unless you are very good at building Legos. Of course, some people like a challenge or a project—you might enjoy building a custom-made bat house yourself. The important thing is to get the house done.

Which Bats to Expect in Your House

Different parts of the United States have different bats. In most of the United States, you might get little brown bats or big brown bats, which often will share a roost in your bat house, especially a big one. If you're lucky and live in a dry part of the country, like the Southwest, you might get pallid bats. These are the light-colored bats that have the neat trick of catching giant centipedes without being stung. Mexican freetails might also move into a bat house in the South or Southwest.

Once the bats are living in the house, you should find out if a group in your town wants you to keep track of the kind and number of bats you have. You don't want to disturb the bats often, but a quick check a few times a year with a flashlight could give useful information about the bats in your area. You can also join the Bat House Research Program at BCI, which collects data on bat houses from around the country (see the If You Want to Know More section for how to join). When the bats have left their house for the winter, check it for any repairs that are needed and clear out any wasp nests.

TUCKED IN TIGHT
Little brown myotis bats (*Myotis lucifugus*) squeeze
into rows in bat houses in a barn in Stayton, Oregon.

What to Do if the Bats Don't Move In

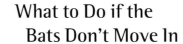

Bats may move into the house you've built for them right away, or they may take as long as a year to three years to move in. Sometimes the bats just won't live in a bat house, even though you think you've done everything right. If you don't get bats in your house, you can try setting the house in another spot. Maybe where you had it, the house was too warm or too cold. The house might need to be painted another color to change the temperature inside. You can contact the organization that sold you the house or plans for advice (see the If You Want to Know More section).

You might also investigate if bat experts live in your town. This can be done by asking your parents to figure it out—they know more adults than you do. You can also contact the US Fish and Wildlife office or state game and fish office in your area for helpful information about bats.

If You Want to Know
More about Bats . . .

Bat Organizations

Bat Conservation International (BCI), www.batcon.org

Bat Conservation International began in 1982, and since then, the organization, founded and headed by Dr. Merlin Tuttle, has continued to champion bats around the world. Whatever you want to know about bats, you'll find it on the BCI website. This is a fun website to just troll around. Headlines guide you to the latest news about bats, and more than 75,000 photographs show you bats flying, zapping bugs, roosting, and being bats in every way. The bats are so strange, exotic, and beautiful that checking out the BCI photos is as fascinating as flipping through the zany images of the universe on NASA's Hubble Telescope site. The BCI website is also excellent for searching out information on a certain kind of bat, like if a bat can be found in your state.

The Bat House Research Program at BCI collects information on bats from bat house owners. This information is then used to keep track of how many bats and what kinds are in different parts of the country and to design new bat houses. You can get involved by going to the BCI website and clicking on Bat Houses or calling (512) 327-9721. Bat houses and plans, including *The Bat House Builder's Handbook*, can be purchased from BCI online at www.batcon.org.

BCI's online catalog sells books and DVDs on bats and very cool posters, including one of 38 bat species in color from around the world. The catalog also tells you how you can adopt a bat for about $35 and what you'll get—not just complete information about the bat species but also a photo, an "endearing letter from your bat," and a "Batty about Bats" bumper sticker.

Fun toys for sale from BCI include a bat kite with an eight-foot (2.4-meter) wingspan for about $40. A great electronic toy is a mini–television camera for watching and listening in on bats at night. You get the camera, a microphone, and 100 feet of cable, then set up the camera and microphone near the bats and plug the cable into your TV, VCR, or computer. But beware: this getup costs about $80. For about $270, you can order a bat detector that will fit in the palm of your hand and pick up different frequencies of bat cries. Some of these bat toys might cost more than your allowance, but try to turn your parents into bat lovers.

Organization for Bat Conservation (OBC), www.batconservation.org

The Organization for Bat Conservation is another bat conservation organization and maintains a staff of field biologists to research endangered bats. The website summarizes current research efforts and lists donations needed to help the bats, like mealworms and pet carriers. If your vacation takes you near Indiana, the yearly OBC bat festival is in Terre Haute and features talks about bats and different kinds of live bats to see. If you want to give bats a home but don't enjoy a big shop at Lowe's for lumber, OBC will sell you a bat house kit to put together. Then all you have to do is buy the parts for the pipe the house stands on. (You can also order free plans for a single-room bat house at www.batcon.org.) If you have questions about building your bat house or getting bats in it, you can contact OBC at www.batroost.com or (248) 645-3232. The OBC has a fun store, with bat photographs, beanie bats, bat screen savers, and lots else.

Bat World Sanctuary, www.batworld.org

Like OBC and BCI, Bat World Sanctuary has it all about bats—species information, what to do if you find a bat in your house or out, how to adopt a bat, and a Bat Bazaar, where you can buy bat books and nice T-shirts. On the very serious side, the website has a "Wall of Shame," listing people and organizations that truly hurt bats. It's hard to look at the horrible pictures in the Wall of Shame, but maybe it's not a bad idea as a reality check.

US Fish and Wildlife Service, www.fws.gov/

The US Fish and Wildlife Service is run by the federal government. It has the splendid mission of "working with others to conserve, protect, and enhance fish, wildlife, and plants and their habitats for the continuing benefit of the American people." The website has links to birds, fishing, endangered species, and much more. If you want to know what the Endangered Species Act *really* said or how the population of a rare animal is doing, the Fish and Wildlife Service site is the place to look. A kids' section guides you to other organizations that save different kinds of wildlife in different parts of the country and even offers to help you with your homework.

Books

Bats in Question, by Don E. Wilson
(order through www.batcon.org, any bookstore)
If you suddenly come up with a question about bats, this book will answer it. *Bats in Question* is divided into three parts: "Bat Facts," "Bat Evolution and Diversity," and "Bats and Humans," and under each part is a list of questions, ranging from "How fast can bats fly?" to "What should I do if I find a sick bat?" The book includes gorgeous, striking photos by Merlin Tuttle, the founder of Bat Conservation International, of bats in flight, eating, and hanging out.

America's Neighborhood Bats, by Merlin D. Tuttle
(order through www.batcon.org, any bookstore)
By the founder of Bat Conservation International, *America's Neighborhood Bats* introduces you to some of your *other* neighbors, with full-color photos of many different kinds of bats and lots of information on common bat neighbors. Sections on the value of bats and conservation give hard facts and numbers. The book has a how-to section for catching a bat loose in your house (a paper towel roll can be useful for scooping it up) and funny (or not-so-funny) stories of what happens when human and bat neighbors don't get along—one woman burned down her house while trying to fry a bat with a flamethrower.

Bats in the Pantry,
by Bat World Sanctuary
(order through www.batworld.org,
www.batconservation.org,
www.batcon.org, any bookstore)
This book is full of recipes—
for everything from salads
to chocolate banana pie—
that include ingredients
made possible by bats. We
wouldn't have bananas or a
whole lot of other good food
without bats—many spices and
vegetables and even chocolate depend on them. The bats pollinate the
plants, spread the seeds, or eat the insects that destroy the plants. The people at
Bat World Sanctuary, who wrote the recipe book, feel very strongly about saving
bats—and what's surprising is that most of the rest of us don't feel that way too. In
our defense, often we just don't know enough about bats to realize how much we
need them. The book points out ingredients that are bat related with a bat sign,
and a glossary in the back explains how bats help to provide that ingredient.

Bats at the Beach, written and illustrated by Brian Lies (order through
www.batcon.org, www.batconservation.org, any bookstore)
Okay, this book is for little kids. But it's too funny and cute to pass up. A family of
bats head to the beach for an outing—but at night, of course. The bats pack banjos
and moon-tan lotion and fly each other as kites while a couple of old bats snooze
in beach chairs. Sounds familiar, right?

Glossary

biosphere: Living organisms and their environment.

carnivore: A group of *mammals*, including wolves, dogs, bears, and cats, that eat meat. A few plants capture and eat insects and are also carnivores.

colony: A group of a *species* that is separate from other groups. Vampire bats form colonies of about 20 bats next to colonies of other kinds of bats, like Mexican freetails.

conserve: To protect and preserve a natural resource, like bats or a clean river.

echolocation: The way bats search out *prey* using sound waves. Bats bounce the sound waves off insects and other prey and can tell by the change in the returning sound waves where the prey is.

ecosystem: A group of living creatures and their *environment*.

environment: What affects a plant or an animal. Light, rainfall, and *predators* are all part of the plant's or animal's environment.

evolution: A change in what *genes* are in a *population* over time.

extinct: When the last member of a *species* dies off, that species is extinct.

food web: In an ecosystem, energy and materials flow around in a web from plants to animals. Plants get energy from the sun and materials from the soil to grow, and then animals get energy and materials to grow by eating plants and each other. Finally decomposers, like fungi, break down dead plants and animals and recycle the materials into soil, ready to be made into new plants and animals.

fossil: What is left of a plant or animal or its outline preserved in rock. Sometimes a bat bone turns to rock itself, or it may just press into a softer substance around it that then turns to rock, leaving an outline.

frequency: The number of electromagnetic waves, like sound waves, that pass a point per unit of time.

gene: A stretch of DNA that controls the inheritance of a trait, like blue eyes or red hair.

global warming: The rise in temperature of the earth's oceans and air resulting from pollution. Greenhouse gases, like carbon dioxide, trap heat and warm the planet.

hibernate: To spend the winter in a resting state. A hibernating animal's body temperature drops to almost the temperature of its *environment*.

isotope: A slightly different version of a chemical element, like carbon, that has different physical properties from other versions of that element.

larva: An early form of an animal that is much different from the adult form. A caterpillar is the larval form of a butterfly and a tadpole is the larval form of a frog.

mammal: A class, or category, of animals. All mammals have fur or hair, feed their young milk, and are *warm blooded*.

megabat: A bat in the suborder Megachiroptera, a group of large bats that eat or drink fruit, nectar, or pollen. Megabats have a claw on their second finger and use their eyes and sense of smell to find food. These bats are also called flying foxes.

microbat: A bat in the suborder Microchiroptera, a group of small bats that mostly eat insects but may eat or drink fruit, nectar, or pollen. Microbats also eat frogs, fish, or blood. These bats echolocate to find food.

migrate: To travel from one place to another to find food or a warmer or colder climate.

mutate: To make a stable change in a plant's or animal's *genes*.

nocturnal: Active at night. Bats, rats, and cats are nocturnal. People are diurnal, or active during the day (except for night owls).

organism: A living being. All plants and animals are organisms.

parasite: A plant or animal that takes advantage of another plant or animal. Ticks are often parasites on dogs—they drink the dogs' blood but do nothing to help the dogs.

pesticide: A chemical used to kill insects or other animals that prey on crops or people.

pollinate: To spread the pollen, or fine dust, from one plant to another so that the plant can reproduce.

population: A group of animals or plants that belong to the same *species.*

predator: An animal that eats or destroys another animal. Some plants eat insects and so can also be called predators.

prey: The food of a *predator.* Insects are one kind of bat prey.

Slavic: A language, like Romanian, that belongs to a group of European languages, including Czech, Polish, Russian, and Bulgarian.

species: A group of animals or plants that are enough alike to breed and have young. A Mexican free-tailed bat can't breed with a vampire bat, and so the two kinds of bats are different species.

tropics: The area north and south of the equator, 23½ degrees north or south in latitude. The tropics are warm and often have thick forests.

warm blooded: To have a body temperature that stays the same no matter what the outside temperature is. Mammals are all warm blooded, but animals like fish and lizards are cold blooded and take on the temperature of their *environment.*

Illustration Credits

Front cover: © J. Scott Altenbach.

Back cover: © J. Scott Altenbach.

endsheets: Illustration by Mary Sundstrom.

page i: Illustration by Mary Sundstrom.

pages ii–iii: Photo © J. Scott Altenbach.

page viii: Photo © Ronal C. Kerbo.

pages 2–3: Photos © J. Scott Altenbach.

page 4: National Park Service photo.

page 5: Illustration by Mary Sunstrom.

pages 6–7: Photo by Merlin D. Tuttle, Bat Conservation International.

page 8: NPS photo by Arvid Aase of FOBU specimen.

page 10: Illustration by Kathleen Sparkes.

page 11: Illustrations by Mary Sundstrom.

page 12: Photo by Merlin D. Tuttle, Bat Conservation International.

page 13: Illustrations by Mary Sundstrom; photo © J. Scott Altenbach.

pages 14–15: Illustrations by Mary Sundstrom.

page 16: Courtesy Library of Congress, control no. 22002725182.

page 17: *HMS* Beagle *in the seaways of Tierra del Fuego*, Conrad Martens, 1831-36, public domain.

page 18: Photo by Merlin D. Tuttle, Bat Conservation International.

page 20: Illustration by Mary Sundstrom; photos by Merlin D. Tuttle, Bat Conservation International.

page 21: Illustration by Mary Sundstrom.

page 22: Photo © J. Scott Altenbach.

page 23: Photo © J. Scott Altenbach.

pages 24–25: Photo © J. Scott Altenbach.

pages 26, 27: Photos by Dianne Odegard. Used with permission.

page 28: Illustration by Mary Sundstrom.

page 29: Photo by Merlin D. Tuttle, Bat Conservation International.

page 30: Photo © J. Scott Altenbach.

page 31/96: Illustration by Mary Sundstrom.

page 32: Photo by Arno, GNU free documentation license.

page 33: Photo © J. Scott Altenbach.

pages 34, 35: Photos © Dan Taylor.

page 36: Photo © J. Scott Altenbach.

page 38: Photo by Merlin D. Tuttle, Bat Conservation International; illustration by Mary Sundstrom.

page 39: Reproduced with permission from John van Wyhe, ed., *The Complete Works of Charles Darwin Online* (http://darwin-online.org.uk/).

page 41: Photo © J. Scott Altenbach.

page 42: Photo © J. Scott Altenbach.

page 43: Illustration by Mary Sundstrom.

page 44: Photos © J. Scott Altenbach.

page 45: Image courtesy of the Granger Collection.

page 46: Photo by Merlin D. Tuttle, Bat Conservation International.

page 48: Illustration by Kathleen Sparkes.

page 49: Illustrations by Mary Sundstrom.

page 50: Illustration by Mary Sundstrom.

page 51: Illustration by Mary Sundstrom.

page 52: Photo by Merlin D. Tuttle, Bat Conservation International.

page 54: Photo © J. Scott Altenbach.

page 55: Photo © J. Scott Altenbach.

page 56: Photo by Ed Arnett, Bat Conservation International.

page 58: Illustration by Mary Sundstrom.

page 61: Illustration by Mary Sundstrom.

pages 62/74: Photo © Warner Bros./PhotoFest.

page 64: Photo by Merlin D. Tuttle, Bat Conservation International; illustration by Mary Sundstrom.

page 65: Charles Livingston Bull, 1918; first published in *Old Crow and His Friends*, Katherine B. Judson, Little, Brown & Co., 1918. Courtesy Library of Congress, control no. cai1996000442/PP.

page 67: Elizabeth Shippen Green, 1902. First published in "*Our Tree-Top Library*," Richard Le Gallienne, *Harper's Magazine*, 1902. Courtesy Library of Congress, control no. cai 1996001490/PP.

pages 68–71: Illustrations by Mary Sundstrom.

page 72: Image from the movie *Nosferatu*, public domain.

page 73: © Producers Releasing Corporation.

page 76: Photo by Mark Kiser, Bat Conservation International.

page 77: Illustration by Mary Sundstrom.

page 79: Photo by Karen Taschek.

pages 80–81: Photo by Merlin D. Tuttle, Bat Conservation International.

page 82: Illustration by Mary Sundstrom.

page 86: Illustration by Mary Sundstrom.

Bat silhouettes appearing throughout the book: Mary Sundstrom.

Welcome to

Worlds of Wonder
A Children's Science Series

Advisory Editors: David Holtby and Karen Taschek

In these engagingly written and beautifully illustrated books,

the University of New Mexico Press seeks to convey to

young readers the thrill of science as well as to inspire further

inquiry into the wonders of scientific research and discovery.

Index

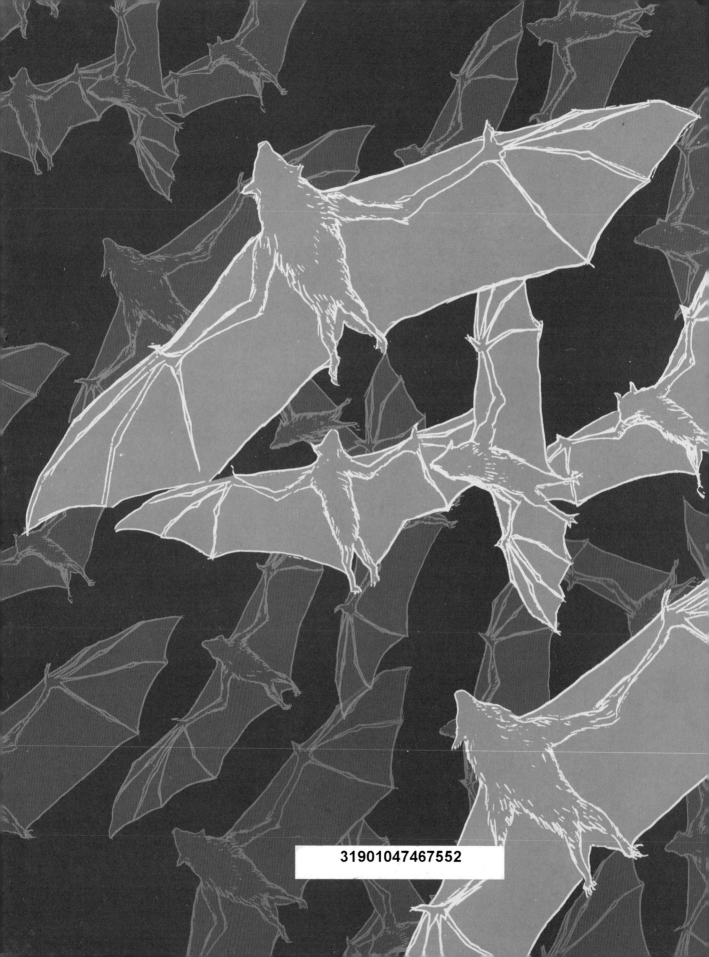

31901047467552